Justice for all

James K. Uphoff, Ed.D.

authorHOUSE®

AuthorHouse™
1663 Liberty Drive
Bloomington, IN 47403
www.authorhouse.com
Phone: 1 (800) 839-8640

Published by AuthorHouse 12/06/2017

ISBN: 978-1-5462-1904-0 (sc)
ISBN: 978-1-5462-1902-6 (hc)
ISBN: 978-1-5462-1903-3 (e)

Library of Congress Control Number: 2017918155

Print information available on the last page.

CHAPTER INDEX

PREFACE

Prior to reading this book on our national system of justice and how many of its interconnected elements must be given attention, the reader needs to know more about me, the author. This introduction will share key elements from my life—its joys and its near tragic event which actually stimulated the book.

Growing Up

I was born in 1937 on September 1, the second of two boys for my parents. Brother Bob was almost 8 ½ years old so I grew up more like an only child but with a highly talented and very good cornet player in the band. Growing up I was much less talented in athletics and was directed to play the clarinet by the band director. I found school to be a challenge for the first three to four months of each year as I was the youngest in my class until the farm kids joined us in high school's ninth grade. But one's life script was well defined by that point.

Our small county-seat town had a seemingly very good social climate so there was very little difficulty for me other than sports. But even there, I found that keeping the score book in baseball was a good alternative to playing and I was respected by teammates. Grades five and seven were more difficult for me as my mouth, which was never an absent part of me gave me troubles.

By the time I was in fifth grade, my brother was gone from home attending college with majors in physics and engineering which served him very well when he enlisted in the Air Force after two years of college. After his basic training in Texas, he was sent to Mississippi for training in basic radar. He graduated top of his class and remained there for the rest of his enlistment as an Instructor of the course. We were all very proud of his success. And I benefited by several vacation trips to the South at Easter time to visit him.

Socially, I was well accepted by a diverse group of my classmates as we did all know each other quite well and many of us were in the same church so even the farm kids were involved. Throughout grades 8-12 at the high school, I was often elected to such positions as Class Secretary or Class Treasurer—but never to any other leadership role. I was socially accepted and did some dating, but never had a 'steady' relationship. Our Class of '55 was the largest for many years but were in Class B, the second largest schools in the state.

From eighth grade on I was a Student Manager for our coaches and ran the clock/score board for all basketball games. I lettered in Track-Field and went to the State Track meet as a miler. My coaches appreciated my abilities as Manager and I found more acceptance. Our school's social climate was very good and quite diverse. I fit in well!

During my Junior year of high school, my brother returned home to finish his own college career. His was around 25 and drove a Mercury red/white car. He was a BMOC (Big Man On Campus) and an excellent student as well. He was a good student and very popular.

I had planned to go to the same small four-year college where our Uncle had taught, but I selected another similar college so that I did not have to compete with his status there.

College Years + Teaching

My four years of college were fun and full of learning. I earned a degree with majors in both history and in geography along with two minors: English and Political Science. That type of course-work also included all the Education courses needed to become qualified as a teacher.

I was in the band, sang in our local church choir, substituted in the Elementary Physical Education program in the school system AND was trained to be a Water Safety Instructor by the local Red Cross which I did for the next four years in their Summer Program.

Obviously I attended school for all four full years but enjoyed all the work. During my junior year I was the Boys Physical Director at the YMCA and still worked as a substitute teacher during the year. I also was much involved in the college's theater program both on-stage and back-stage. I dated some but again never had a "girl-friend" steady relationship but had dates for all major dances.

I graduated in 1959 and took a job in central Nebraska teaching and coaching at a grade 7-9 Junior High School. I also coached football, basketball, and track for several years until I began to officiate both football and basketball which I did for many years. I taught grade seven English and Social Studies to two groups of seventh graders for six years. Because I was an excellent teacher and my students including those with the less reading abilities were able to do much better than they had in elementary schools, I became the Group Leader for this assignment. In subsequent years I assigned myself to teach mostly the lower level pupils who would today have been in special education classes. Again, more success was evident which gave me a background in this special field.

My wife to be was a native of this large city (35,000) returned there to teach at my same building following her graduation from her Sioux Falls, SD college. Her background in both History and English as well as Music in keyboard and vocal gave her a strong background for teaching in the same building where I was now in my third year. We dated, became engaged, and then married in August, 1962 and have now reached our 55th Anniversary. We moved to Lincoln in June 1965.

We both received our Master's Degrees at the University of Nebraska in Secondary Education which enabled us both to take graduate courses in our teaching fields as well as more education course work. I included courses in History, Geography, Economics, English, and Reading which enriched my content fields greatly. My doctoral degree was a continuation of the Master's level program. The Ed.D. program was complete in June, 1967 which led to a move to Dayton, OH in time to begin my career at Wright State University yet that summer as the only professor of social studies education. Harriet taught in grade nine English and Social Studies at Fairborn, OH.

45 Years of College Work: Summary

Starting as an Assistant Professor of Education at age 29, but with 6 years of public school teaching experience and 2 years as an Instructor at University level, I was the only person within our new and rapidly growing institution to have such credentials. By 1971 I was promoted to Associate Professor with tenure. I worked extensively with fellow faculty in Liberal Arts given my own strong background.

My wife and I decided that it was now time to begin our own family. We tried without success, took tests, and were very open to such a change in our lives. Success avoided our best efforts.

Working with Dr. Nick Piediscalzi, Chairman of Religion Department, we co-founded and then co-directed the Public Education Religion Studies Center (PERSC). We traveled across the U.S. to explain how one can only help children to understand the world IF one also teaches ABOUT how religion serves people, their beliefs and cultures. I had taught this way even before the Supreme Court said that we should be doing it this way in 1963.

Within the College of Education and Human Services I had long been teaching graduate courses off-campus at the requests of local school districts. They told us what their needs were and I designed a course to meet their needs. This included several such courses at the Lake Campus of WSU including two different summer sessions. In 1974 I was selected to be the Dean of Branch Campuses moved in September to the Celina-St.Marys location.

I was then in charge of ALL courses offered at the Campus, registration, admissions, bursar, and farming of almost 100 acres of ground owned by the Advisory Council---a diverse role for certain. After much success including me teaching one course in American History while that prof was on leave, I was finding this administrative role to be a fit one for me. I was promoted to full Professor status.

Suddenly we found ourselves to be 'expecting' a child in Fall 1978. This changed our lives dramatically. My wife's doctoral studies program at the Ohio State University had to be dropped. She returned to teaching English in Troy, OH in January 1979 and I decided to return to faculty status in Dayton. We became parents, Harriet at age 38 and me at age 40.

Nicholas James was born on October 3, 1978 just beyond the starting school date in Ohio—more on this later. We loved this new person in our family; we adored his arrival. When I returned to the Dayton campus and my faculty position I was immersed in teaching and fatherhood. As the years progressed friends and others seemed to be surprised when we rejected their suggestions to have him tested and begin school a year early. My own school and social experiences as a very young child said we should not push.

My own research efforts did take a dramatic turn as I switched to interest in age at school entrance and seeking what correlations existed in terms of later success. My first major book, SUMMER CHILDREN: READY OR NOT FOR SCHOOL was co-authored with a School Psychologist, and an English teacher. The book sold and went through 6 printings! Several other books on Kindergarten policies, early childhood, and school systems followed. Then two editions of a book presenting the case for adding an early year experience without failing and citing dozens of studies done all over the nation on this issue were added.

I enjoyed teaching again, but in January 1981 was appointed to the open position as Director of Educational Field Experiences. I served in this very significant pre- and student teaching experience bringing improved planning and programming into the program. In March 1991 I was informed by the Dean that I was to be replaced. Shocked, hurt, dismayed---all were present but I returned to my main love---classroom teaching with vigor. A stroke in summer 1993 took me out for part of a year, but my love of teaching re-invigorated me even by Winter, 1994 when I co-taught an off-campus course for cooperating teachers in a single school district. Much enjoyment for the students involved and for us—the faculty.

The Dean (same man who fired me previously) was now convinced that I was very supportive of his new program and was the best person to replace the current Chair of Teacher Education who was taking a one-year leave. With some concerns in my mind, I took the position offer and enjoyed it until I retired from teaching in 1997. But in Spring of that year, the University Promotion and Tenure Committee selected me as the Outstanding Professor for my excellence in teaching, scholarship, and service to the University. A major honor for me!

Retirement to Half-time Work

Although I was retired I did not leave WSU. I continued to teach part time there and at University of Dayton and Antioch University. In January I applied for a half-time position as Associate Director of the WSU Center for Teaching and Learning responsible for faculty development across the university. Covered by the University insurance program, I did not need to fully retire until a new Provost undertook to make major changes in the CTL program.

Prior to his actions I had many good experiences working with faculty from across the campus on such aspects as 1. Visiting faculty in their own classrooms, collecting observation data, and sharing it with them; 2. Going to a faculty class and collecting and then tallying mid-term student feedback followed by sharing the results with them; 3. Working with faculty on course design, development, and learning via workshops, seminars, etc.; and 4. Assisting our staff with appropriate design of classrooms being changed/enlarged.

I had much time available for my other interests and this led to me collecting and saving examples of child porn and even helping writers edit some of their efforts in this field. Access to good copiers, older but good computers, and a misplaced feeling that I could use such material to help teachers and professors to better prepare future teachers to counter such material led me over the next years to commit the crime of possessing child porn myself.

While this action becoming known caused me great embarrassment and essentially, I felt at least, destroyed my reputation and long quality career. As I have had to confront this major error in my thought process, I have given much time to prayer about and for the unknown youth whose lives I might have made much tougher.

I have had trouble becoming re-established in a church having been rebuffed directly in two congregations and just never felt I could return to my home church. My home Pastor was very supportive of me and even visited me while I was in federal prison. But he retired from the ministry and left that church. A life-long Lutheran I found it hard to reconnect and my wife as a very strong member of the Lutheran church was equally wounded by my actions and the reactions to me.

My wife and I have now re-established a very solid church relationship. I have again been asked to help with communion distribution. We celebrated our 55th Anniversary with this large Christian church and are very comfortable with this congregation's many programs and outreaching to others. At our ages now, we are unable to be as active as we once were, but we find it to be a good home and we have not missed any Sundays!

My prayers about and for the youth whose pictures I downloaded and saved remain in my most significant thoughts today. What I have done has shown me true friends who have been able to look beyond the painful thing I had done and to support fully my "re-entry" into life. My fellow faculty member—a history professor with whom I went on a trip to Iraq and the United Arab Emirates in the Middle East in 1989—wrote me letters and even visited me once while I was in prison in 2013-14.

Such support and help was crucial to me as I have tried to return to an active life while on parole since my release after thirteen+ months of incarceration. An English professor as well as a retired Professor of Theater Arts are two more examples of 'forgiving' men whose friendship has proven to be valuable to me personally.

A call to me in mid-September, 2015 reached me at the Prison. Our son was calling to Inform me that my wife/his mother had suffered a stroke and was in the hospital. He was flying home from North Carolina to be with her for as long as necessary. NO early release was possible for me, so I had to resort to the only current support system I had. The Catholic priest and my friends I was teaching in the GED program at the prison were great!

When my son drove to the prison to bring me home upon my release in November 2015, he told me a lot about how his mother was doing, how many people had called upon her when she was in rehab, and his expectations for her future health. Throughout the time before he had to return to North Carolina, he became a very strong support pillar for me. My appreciation to her and him for their much forgiveness and help!

Conclusion

It is this story and my many long-lasting relationships which have enabled me to research and write this book. My prime hope is that given the anti-human approach of our current federal, state, local leadership in the fields of justice and constitutional behaviors can still be turned around. My hope that my extensive use of hundreds of local news accounts and stories will prove to those readers who have an open mind and desire **justice for all** will be able to take their own actions for reform. My Judge, who, upon my release, urged me to create this book and has now approved it as having met my community service hours, is now thanked very strongly for his commitment and trust in me.

CHAPTER 1

"Why the words, 'JUSTICE FOR ALL'?"

I began my teaching career in 1959 teaching Social Studies and English for grades seven through nine in a Junior High School. Our daily school ritual back then is still followed by many public schools today. Our local Fox 45 TV station, WRGT 45, airs each day in its morning TV News a tape of a specific class saying their Pledge of Allegiance.

"I pledge allegiance to the flag of the
United States of America and to the
Republic for which it stands, one
Nation under God,
Indivisible, with Liberty
*and **Justice for All**."*

The fundamental question for each one of us boils down to: **"What IS Justice for All?"** Do we really believe that it is such a basic and essential commitment of our own society? The word, 'all', means every one of us **including** those who have been convicted of some crime and then incarcerated. This group of inmates has grown to huge numbers over the past few decades. The implication of that figure is taken from a short article in the November 2, 2015 issue of the *Christian Science Monitor* which described this numbers issue as follows:

> "*The United States is the world's leading incarcerator;* it has less than five percent of the world's population but a quarter of the world's prisoners. Prisons cost states more than $50 billion a year and are second fastest-growing part of state budgets behind Medicaid."

Yet though these citizens may be in jail or prison or out on probation, they are still very much a part of the ALL. This book will be looking at the key question from a variety of perspectives. Some have been the victims of crimes, some have committed crimes, some have worked to bring them to justice, and others have worked to help those who served their time to make a successful re-entry into society. I hope to use my own several life experiences in and among these various groups to assist readers to consider the many aspects of our System and the many efforts to provide a 'YES' answer to the basic question, **"Is our System of Justice really for ALL?"**

I finished my two graduate degrees (1962 and 1967) and became an Education professor with specialties in K-12 Social Studies curriculum. Those degrees included graduate work in History, Geography, Economics and English. Given this academic focus along with the importance of a solid school curriculum and experiences for children from 5 to 19 years of age, my attention to the continuing school routine of reciting the Pledge of Allegiance to the Flag of the United States of America has now 'raised several flags' in my mind.

When reading (and saying) the Pledge, I must ask you to be alert to the use (and non-use) of the comma! You will please note that there is NO comma after the word "nation" BUT orally we add a comma at that spot when we recite the Pledge. OK---I am a purist but I did teach English for six years before moving on to 'professing' in higher education.

Justice for All

Because the Pledge puts that societal goal as the final message point, this book will explore our nation's *System of Justice* as it exists at the most local level via mayor's courts, law enforcement systems from Barney Fife in Mayberry to Federal Marshalls and the FBI at the national level. Judges who are elected (or not), Prosecutors who also must be elected, and public defense attorneys who must please those who appoint them are all subject to the whims and human weaknesses of those who elect or appoint these essential elements of the system.

At one time there was the oft-stated goal of rehabilitation as the purpose of our Justice System. We wanted that those convicted could be re-affiliated into society in a productive contributing way. Has this positive effort been replaced by a growing philosophy of punishing as the prime goal? For too many inmates their long-delayed return (if ever) into society is with no real rehabilitation ever having been made available!

Our daily news brings us vivid evidence of illegal convictions of people who are just now being freed with their convictions overturned. After decades of illegal actions by the system's officials which have deprived them of their freedom, they now are back in society with us. Taxpayers are now having to have their governments pay out millions of dollars *as punishments of* ***the system's malpractices*** *via the courts, the prisons, and/or the medical services* provided or denied to those incarcerated. Not only are there major emotional and/or financial costs to the humans so injured, but also real tax costs out of our collective tax pockets as the System is having now to pay reparations for the misdeeds!

One more brief example of an all too common "judicial malpractice" concerns the very basic tenet of our court system---*trial by a jury of peers*! Peers is commonly defined as people like the defendant. Bryan Stevenson's 2014 book, ***JUST MERCY***, points out that the U.S. Supreme Court has repeatedly found the System to be failing to provide a jury of peers with even a slight representation of African Americans. In the 1880's *Stauder v WV.* decision the Court said this lack was **outside** the Constitution and thus OK. But in 1986, *Batson v Ky,* the Court ruled such lack of peers on juries **was** unconstitutional. Once again but much more recently in *Foster v Ga,* the Court by a 7-1 vote on May 23, 2016 ruled that systematically *removing* peers from a jury IS ALSO UNCONSTITUTIONAL! Justice for All remains a goal which has been much too frequently ignored by the System in many parts of our country!

As we have our children pledge their allegiance to a system of JUSTICE FOR ALL, what will be their confidence in that flag and what it says but is not followed in practice? Will they be encouraged to trust the judicial system? Will they look for ways to scam the system? Will they retreat and isolate themselves in their school work, their lives, and their adult actions on behalf of our nation and society? Or will the current efforts to reform the system be seen to be appropriate and of significant benefit to us all?

There have been many cases of malpractice within the justice system by all levels of it prior to the actual trial and sentencing. This includes cases of local officers turning themselves into prosecutor-judge-jury and *executioner* as they put many bullets into an unarmed person or a choke-hold to death on a man who was selling untaxed cigarettes.

Prosecutors have been found guilty of withholding key evidence from the defense, of not calling witnesses who would agree with the defendant's version of events, of rigging a jury which would render a decision in their favor, AND there have been Judges who went along with such illegal actions. All misdeeds that took place prior to the actual Guilty decision was reached.

Then there is another major element in the system that encompasses the time a person spends as an inmate under forced incarceration. There have been major problems with medical services provided or with-held, of diets that contributed to more medical problems, etc. These problems within the system are less well known to the public, but must be made public and changes made to prevent them from continuing.

Finally, I will also share with you a number of very positive actions that are already in place to address the all-too-troublesome negatives currently being found much too frequently. A look at solid practices should give us all stimulation for becoming an active part in positive efforts to better serve our nation. Punishment does have a place, without a question, but being able to return a felon back into society and able to become a tax-paying contributing member of the community currently is too often found to be seriously missing.

This chapter has been devoted to giving my readers a brief view of the many aspects of the judicial system in our diverse nation. A look at the Table of Contents indicates that each of these problem areas receives direct and special attention. It is my hope that your reading will be both informative and functional.

My goal in writing this book is to help every reader to give serious and thoughtful attention to being fully informed about the failures of the system. My goal is that we will all focus that knowledge by becoming active participants in seeking the essential reforms that will enable our nation to meet the goals of The Pledge as so clearly stated in its final three words: JUSTICE FOR ALL.

James K. Uphoff, Ed.D.
jamesuphoff@twc.com
(937) 567-0955

CHAPTER 2

The Formula: (E + V) = JFA /sq. dl

The formula is much less difficult to understand when our nation more fully understands the vital importance and connection of the election process. How voting impacts the fairness of our Justice for All system and goal is crucial. Elections have very direct impact upon the Justice System. Many crucial leaders in the total system are directly elected by those who are eligible to vote. Thus who is allowed to vote is crucial because those denied the right to vote are also denied the right to help select these significant persons.

Consider how many "justice leaders" are <u>elected</u> to their position. Many local judges as well as those on appeals courts and on State Supreme Courts are elected. Almost all local city or county Attorneys/Prosecutors and state Attorney Generals are really the prosecutors. These elected officials may even appoint Public Defenders. The elected prosecutors have major powers to call Grand Juries, determine which charges, if any, to make against a defendant, and also defend their own jurisdiction if the county or state is sued. Some local law enforcements leaders such as Sheriffs are elected. They oversee the hiring and training of their deputies just as Police Chiefs do in other jurisdictions even though only their elected leaders are a step-removed in the employment and supervision process.

Also elected are those local village, township, city, and county commissioners/trustees. They, along with state legislators hire the local or state law enforcement leaders for their own jurisdictions. These legislators also make the laws and determine the general punishments that accompany the crimes for their own locations. They may also have major roles in the punishment dimension since the jails and prisons of our nation are created and funded by these elected governing bodies.

Another major group of elected officials are the local School Board members who make many decisions about the nature and success of the public school system. They appoint the leaders of their system and hire those recommended by the leaders. Given that some writers address what is being called, "The School to Prison Pipeline," * the elected Board of Education members are responsible for a significant part of our society and thus too often, also its juvenile Judicial System. All members of our society should seriously be involved in the local elections of school board members.

**Too often poor student success in school leads to criminal behavior as if the child is on a 'railroad track' that ends in his/her incarceration. Plus, juvenile prisons offer little real educational help for such students.*

Now if many citizens who are typically fully eligible to vote are suddenly deprived of that precious fundamental right, they are no longer able to play a significant role in any of the actions or levels just cited. Purging voter rolls, limiting the times/places/ways when voters are able to vote and adding new obstacles for voters are actions which very negatively limit the ability of those voters to play a key role in our Justice System.

Historical Changes in Who Can Vote

In our nation's early days only white males who owned property were eligible to vote. Then the property requirement was removed. After the Civil War and especially in the South for decades such new requirements as literacy tests, special taxes, and intimidations were used to limit who could vote. Women have been allowed to vote for only the past century but our nation has generally been making progress toward voting eligibility for all citizens. The more people who are eligible to vote, the stronger our nations justice system will be.

Sidebar: One Vote Counts!

The title of the short story is, *"The Mother Who Saved Suffrage: Passing the 19th Amendment"* by Jennie Cohen. This even shorter version is about the last State to ratify the 19th Amendment to the U.S. Constitution which read"_ the right of citizens of the United States to vote shall not be denied or abridged by the United States or by any State on account of sex." On August 18, 1920 a total of 35 States had ratified, but one more was needed and Tennessee was considering this action. Its Senate had ratified but the House was divided 48-48 and was considering whether or not to say Yes or No and had just defeated a motion to table the vote by 48-48. The youngest member, Harry Burn—age 24, had been on the anti-suffrage (No) side but had just received a note from his mother, Phoebe Ensminger Burg (called Miss Febb by family and friends) strongly supporting the Amendment and urging her son "to be a good boy" and support it as well. He did then vote, Yes! He thus brought about the fury of his House anti-peers "while presumably avoiding that of his mother—which may very well have been the more daunting of the two.... I know that a mother's advice is always safest for her boy to follow....and my mother wanted me to vote for ratification."

ONE VOTE MADE A MAJOR CHANGE IN OUR NATION!

Bernard Grofman wrote in 1990 A Twentieth Century Fund Paper entitled, *Voting Rights, Voting Wrongs, The Legacy of Baker v. Carr (1962).* The case decision by the United States Supreme Court (USSC) ruled that our Constitution mandated the principle of "one-man-one vote." That decision "dramatically changed legislative apportionment in this country." Grofman states that without this decision, *"I believe that the Voting Rights Act of 1965 would have emerged a far weaker document in terms of its enforcement mechanisms."* Each person should be able to vote and have that vote count equally across districts for congressional and state elections.

But still today well into the second decade of the 2000s, our nation continues to deal with very explicit attempts to control the voting process. Meeting and furthering political goals of a party in control is being used to turn the voting public into numbers more likely to favor that party. This was encouraged when the USSC (2013) eased the mandated pre-approval requirements (Section 5) of the Voting Rights Act (Section 2 in 1982 amendments) "that prohibited the use of any electoral device that would have the purpose or effect of diluting minority voting strength."

From then on a number of states have passed laws to restrict dramatically the right to vote. While they claimed to be trying to prevent "voter-fraud", the legislators could provide no examples of there being any such problem. Recently, in 2016 the Federal Courts and even some state courts have been striking down as unconstitutional elements of these recent state voting changes. Citations have included "surgically crafted" actions such as cutting the times for Sunday voting—a practice found more commonly used by black voters.

The December 20, 2015 issue of the New York Times article by Jim Rutenberg led with the following title and summary: *"BLOCK THE VOTE After the 2013 Supreme Court decision that gutted the Voting Rights Act, new tactics to suppress minority voting rights are flourishing –especially in states like Texas, where a growing Latino population is reshaping the electorate."*

USA TODAY's August 3, 2016 lead opinion editorial carried the following bold-heading: **"Rulings reveal true agenda behind voter ID laws"** Their key points quickly followed: "*…Yet there is ample reason to applaud rulings from four federal courts in the past two weeks striking down laws in Texas, North Carolina, Wisconsin, and North Dakota that* *could deny hundreds of thousands of potential voters—mostly minorities, often poor or elderly—their most basic right under the Constitution. Taken together, the rulings provide further confirmation that these laws were more about suppressing turnout than about preventing fraud."*

Additional challenges are also before the Courts. Ohio has also drawn attention. The NY Times December 13, 2015 headline read, "Ohio Working to Fix Ballot Problems." A Dayton Daily News story on 12-27-15 was headlined, "Ohio's voting rules suit awaits ruling, Dems objecting to Republican-backed revisions to policy" (Ann Sanner, Associated Press) The lead story in the Dayton Daily News on Sunday, August 7, 2016 was headlined, "Election 2016 Voting Laws put to test in Ohio in 2016, Secretary of state lauds system; lawyer* calls it unconstitutional." (Laura Bischoff, Columbus Bureau) [*former Federal prosecutor]

African-Americans, Latinos, and Native Americans are among the special targets of such attempts to disallow and prevent minorities from being able to vote. One Court called the actions of one state to have been "surgically designed". That state actually showed how they had asked key questions about certain voting options. One example was, "Who votes early most often?" When the answer was "Mostly the Black community and/or the poor," the new law then reduced the early voting options.

In a Monday, October 23, 2017 mailing the Southern Poverty Law Center issued an email announcement that it had filed a suit against a private company, the city of Gardendale, AL and a local Judge over an illegal probation scheme. Both the local municipal Judge and the City Council members were all **elected** officials! The had created for many poverty residents a type of modern day "debtors 'prison" which would be unconstitutional. SPLC has had much success with similar law suits previously. A separate ethics complaint with the Judicial Inquiry Commission of Alabama against the Judge has also been filed for his part in this scheme.

The NAACP has become very concerned about the entire voting/elections system. For example, the Dayton Ohio chapter hosted two very open meetings to solicit public opinion and information about how to make the election process more fair and more effective. One of their concerns was to find out how people make decisions about elections for local or state judges. When it became clear that most folks knew very little about the candidates the discussions turned to how can the organization can help voters become better informed about their choices.

Concerns about the role of voters in a number of different elections from very local (schools, villages, townships, cities, counties, state legislature and state-wide positions, to federal congressional seats and president) all the way to the leadership of our nation are at stake and our Judicial System is involved/ impacted at all levels. As this book examines in more detail the many aspects of the system that are currently under attack, seen as being mal-functioning, and failing to provide Justice for All, then we will be better able to help bring about the needed reforms.

Former Prisoners Also Should VOTE

On Sunday, October 30, 2016 *The New York Times* editorial was very explicit in its call for all prisoners who had by now completed their incarceration should be permitted to vote. Its editorial headline said it all: "Agreed: Serve Your Time, Cast Your Ballot." Given that the current Presidential campaign has produced such widely discrepant views on so many social issues between conservative and liberal Americans, but the important right of "released" felons to be able to vote is NOT AMONG THEM!

In some states former prisoners are fully eligible to vote. For me, Ohio is one of those states, but for many that right may never be extended to those who have served their time and met their obligations to society. This remains a major factor in justice reform across our nations

In a national survey just released in 2016 by the Public Relations Research Institute (PRRI), a nonpartisan opinion research organization, shows that Americans think that people who have committed felonies and paid the price for their crimes should now be able to vote. **But** laws in a dozen states will bar more than three million people from doing exactly that. The report says, "Three-quarters of all Americans, believe that these people deserve the right to participate in democracy, and that support reaches across the political spectrum to include clear majorities of Republicans, Democrats, conservatives, moderates, and liberals." Those surveyed are very supportive of this right to vote.

The chart below shows the breakout of votes by many categories. The numbers represent those agreeing and those disagreeing! (**XXX** vs ZZZ). The percent who agree that a person who has been convicted of a felony and has paid the price for it should be allowed to vote. (Note: Some totals do not quite reach 100%.)

Category	Favor	Oppose
* Republican	62%	38%
* Conservative	62%	38%
* Tea Party	64%	36%
* Ages 65+	65%	34%
* Ages 50-64	69%	30%
* White	71%	28%
* Men	72%	28%
* High School or Less	73%	26%
* Some College	73%	26%
* Independent	73%	26%
* **All Americans**	**74%**	**26%**
* Women	75%	23%
* College graduate	75%	26%
* Post-graduate	76%	24%
* Ages 18-29	78%	20%
* Hispanic	78%	20%
* Politically Moderate	78%	22%
* Ages 30-49	79%	21%
* Democrat	83%	16%
* Liberal	83%	17%
* Black	85%	13%

This collection of figures shows that almost at least two-thirds of all people completing this form have shown a very positive outlook in favor of increased voting for former felons.

I am one of those who is now able to vote. For this I am very grateful because all votes do count and make a difference. Thus the formula title of this chapter is explained.

(E + V) = JFA/sq.dl
(Elections + Voting) = Justice For All /square deal

Being informed about the system and being an active voter in fair elections will enhance the chances of making our Justice System truly FOR ALL!

CHAPTER 3

Police/Community Discord Growing Dramatically

> ***"Hate begets hate; violence begets violence; toughness begets a greater toughness. We must meet the forces of hate with the power of love."* Martin Luther King, Jr.**

Suddenly there is a body just reclining on the street in the middle for hours—dead, shot by one officer. People are shouting, "Hand Up! Don't Shoot!" The white police in this dominantly black community are facing dozens, then hundreds, and then thousands of angry faces. Violence erupts against the now military-looking army of officers facing them. "BLACK LIVES MATTER!" is shouted loudly again and again. The almost all white police force and its almost all white city council members have become the enemy! It is Ferguson, Missouri and this was the spark for much attention for years ahead.

Local and state law enforcement personnel have historically been provided with "extra legal safeguards" for their rights because their job is designed to protect and serve, but their roles are too often subjected to much danger for themselves and others. Such safeguards developed by elected state and federal legislators and signed by elected governors and presidents are being challenged strongly by society today.

What appears to the public to be a typical case of murder or assault in criminal court does not necessarily result even in a charge, let alone a trial and conviction for a law enforcement officer. The standards of proof are stronger in such a case as happened in the Baltimore, MD trials of a number of officers where no jury was involved—only the Judge. Not a one was found guilty in court.

The small report of February 10, 2016 by Kade Crockford of the ACLU Massachusetts was headlined, "This Federal Appeals Court's Ruling Put a Dent in Police Officers' 'Qualified Immunity' Defense." (emphasis added). During a SWAT raid in the early morning hours to check for drugs, a 68 –year old African-American grandfather was accidentally shot to death while lying on his stomach with hands above his head. A closed-case it would seem, but not this time.

Officer Duncan pointed his gun at a non-threatening person, had his finger on the trigger and the safety off. The gun accidentally fired. The First Circuit Court of Appeals ruled that "A police officer is not immune from accountability after he points a gun at a non-threatening person," which then fired. This case, "has far-reaching implications for public safety and police accountability." The Civil Lawsuit will now continue!

Part of the problem is that so many situations find the officers needing to make crucial decisions about the mental health of a person, the status of his "weapon"—real or a child gun, and was he running away or toward the officer. Very little training has ever been given for the men and women in blue to cope quickly and adequately with such issues. Thus they have had "extra safeguards" (Qualified Immunity) provided for them. But, how many safeguards and how should the law enforcement agents of our nation be expected to respond? This is the real issue and the answers are not clear.

Other Factors

Another key factor involves the role of the Prosecutor. Typically, the local Prosecutor has an extended and close working relationship with his/her local law enforcement personnel. The role of the Prosecutor will be the focus of a later chapter, but one of the changes being used in some places in our Justice System is for the Prosecutor to quickly **recuse** him/herself from this local case and seek a prosecutor from well-outside the offence- jurisdiction.

Our very diverse American society in terms of race, ethnicity, wealth, religion, sexual orientation, age, etc. has been a crucial factor in how justice is perceived. When the police force is over 90% majority and its city is over 50% minority, problems are very likely to be found. Now add in the significant problems of poverty, joblessness, school failures, and lack of medical/mental health care and you have the start of a major inferno.

Nick Romeo wrote the Christian Science Monitor's August 6, 2016 review of Nancy Isenberg's book, *White Trash. The 400-Year Untold History of Class in America.* He provides some key insights into the growing distrust between society and local law enforcement as her book looks at poverty. Such lower-economic status often is racial in nature and includes many minorities, newly arrived immigrants, and non-whites as well. Native Americans have also experienced these problems for many years.

His opening paragraph sets Isenberg's historical look at America's social goals—targets often missed even though desired at least in words. *"In 1786, Thomas Jefferson articulated a founding myth of American democracy. '[I]n America, no distinction between man and man had ever been known…poorest laborer stood on equal ground with the wealthiest millionary."* Her book looks at the rebranding of white trash as an ethnic identity. Such poorer whites may have too often been the most likely to find the KKK and other hate groups as representing the frustrations of white poverty. These too often are found in the mixed-reactions of society to police actions.

To the extent that recruits for police and prison guards have often been from less well-educated, more blue collar backgrounds, the makeup of our nation's law enforcers has been a factor in the problems of police/community relations today. For example, prison guards in the Federal system need only have a high school education or GED. The same has been true for local law enforcement in some places. The ability to think and reason and adjust to change and create constructive options have not been prominent in the previous experiences of too many of these recruits.

DOJ Investigation: Baltimore

On August 10,2016 the Department of Justice presented its final report on the Investigation of the Baltimore City Police Department. The Executive Summary of this lengthy and scathing report documents in detail four prime problems: "(1) Making unconstitutional stops, searches, and arrests; (2) Using enforcement strategies that produce severe and unjustified disparities in the rates of stops, searches and arrests of African Americans; (3) Using excessive force, and (4) Retaliating against people engaging in constitutionally-protected expression. This pattern or practice is driven by systemic deficiencies in BPD's policies, training, supervision, and accountability structures that fail to equip officers with the tools they need to police effectively and within the bounds of the federal law." On a CNN news report this same day, BPD Commissioner K. Davis stated that already some officers are no longer on the force and new actions for training and supervision are 'in the works.'

Technological Changes

One of the major new elements in the world of policing has been the huge expansion of technology. With portable phones that take still pictures and make video recordings, the words of a witness and of an officer are being challenged as never before. Now the expansion and use of dashboard and body cameras (if they don't fall off the body or don't work for the officer that actually fired the shot—real events) have given the public 'evidence' that the police rarely had to accommodate. Additionally, equipment 'failures' add more fuel to the growing fire of distrust and disbelief.

The Week, July 29, 2016 entitled its page 18 article, "Live Streaming: Facebook Live's distressing breakthrough." The magazine's own words are very descriptive. "'...you may well have watched someone die---possibly at the exact moment it happened,' said Issie Lapowsky in ***Wired.com***. First, the world watched as Diamond Reynolds used Facebook Live to broadcast her boyfriend Philando Castile's final moments after police shot him during a traffic stop (for a missing tail light) in Falcon Heights, Minn. The very next night, real-time footage of the shooting rampage that killed five police officers in Dallas flooded onto Facebook newsfeeds before it was picked up by cable news networks.... Now these (types of) images come fast, furious, and unfiltered."

When such visual evidence is suddenly available to millions of people world-wide, public emotions are easily aroused. But when some locations (Chicago?) wait months and months before releasing their own films, public trust turns to DIStrust quickly. Demonstrations begin and grow as not only local folks want to make their concerns heard while agitators from far away often arrive to agitate and disrupt.

Controlling such constitutionally-protected free speech and demonstration becomes a new and very complicated role for law enforcement. Recently the use of heavy armored former military equipment and tactics almost always exacerbates the situation into violent encounters and property destruction. Calls for **BLACK LIVES MATTER** speak loudly of the vividly perceived unlawful killing of Black males by local police/sheriffs. This, in turn, has stimulated a few to take individual actions to return these killings by now targeting the police. (Dallas, Baton Rouge). EXPLOSION TIME IS NOW WITHIN LARGER SOCIETY!

The tragedy in Dallas was especially hurtful to those seeking a healing between citizens and police because the Dallas police had just marched alongside the protestors of the Louisiana and Minnesota police killings of Black males. There were no conflicts during the march and the protestors seemed to be very comfortable with the personal and friendly way in which the Dallas police were just walking there alongside them—*no tanks, armored police with shields, etc.* Then the single gunner began killing policemen! This was followed just days later by a man from Missouri coming to Louisiana to kill three more policemen. ***Dr. King's words are still relevant, perhaps even more so today.*** *" Hate, violence and toughness have all done their 'begetting'! We now have a major question before us!*

Can the River of Discontent Be Bridged?

There are many costs incurred when this river is in flood stage. The following is a list of specific Black Male deaths by law enforcement which never had a trial with a guilty verdict except for the one on the list. All of the other results came via Civil Trial or Jurisdiction reaching an out-of-court civil agreement with families. The bottom line is to see the huge amount of taxpayer and/or insurance dollars that the public law enforcement **mal**practices had incurred.

Recent 'Resolutions' involving Police-Involved Deaths of Black Males

- Baltimore, MD — Freddie Gray, $6.4 million
- Chicago, IL — Laquan McDonald, $5 million
- Chicago, IL — Flint Farmer, $4.1 million
- Cincinnati, OH — Sam DuBose, $5.3 million
- Cleveland, OH — Tamir Rice, $5.6 million
- Cleveland, OH — Kenny Smith $5.5 million **(via a jury case)**
- Los Angeles, CA — Brian Beard, $5 million
- New York City, NY — Eric Gardner, $5.9 million
- N. Charleston, SC — Walter Scott, $6.5 million
- Oxnard, CA — Alfonso Limon, $6.7 million

On Sunday, July 31, 2016, Mark Gokavi's major front page story in the Dayton Daily News focused on the 2-year old shooting of a Black male by a Beavercreek white officer. While no charges or even firing of the officer has taken place, the story's' large headline read, "Officer's use of force 10 times the average." Within that story were key facts about the dollar costs to public government bodies for other similar cases of police killing of Black males. Please note the huge amounts of dollars of tax money spent as out-of-court settlements or in one case by court order.

A more recent shooting of a young Black male by a police officer resulted in major rioting, violence, burning, and looting—Milwaukee, WI –mid-August 2016. Leonard Pitts, Jr., an African-American columnist for the *Miami Herald,* analyzed this major event in his August 21, 2016 column. Sylville Smith, 23, had a lengthy arrest record—drugs, weapons, robbery—but he ran from a traffic stop. When ordered to stop, he quickly turned around, gun in hand. The African-American police officer (age 24) shot and killed Sylville.

Pitts describes the situation as follows. "Blacks in Wisconsin's largest city say Smith's death was the last straw after years of racially stratified policing. It is hardly immaterial that an officer was not charged just two years ago in the controversial shooting death of a mentally ill black man. Or that the department is under Justice Department review which, to its credit it requested."

Many studies have found, "…patterns of institutionalized racism that corrode public trust and impinge the ability of police to do their jobs." The column ends with this agonizing assessment. "This violence, following what might well have been a justified shooting, was tragic and troubling. But it also made one thing starkly clear. Blacks have been demanding justice a long time. And they're getting tired of asking nicely."

Dollars alone do not rebuild bridges of lost trust, confidence, fairness, and hope for real and lasting improvement by all. Baltimore's task ahead is massive because the scope and depth of the police department's problems are so significant. But the Dallas Chief of Police was so strongly commended for how their law enforcement has made so many improvements. It can be done and as the new Chief for Ferguson, MO said in a TV interview, "We hope others can look to us and to Dallas for what we have done and are still doing so that others need not experience the problems that put us on the headlines."

A Chicago Story—sad but with some hope for Justice

On October 20, 2014 in the city's Southwest side Officer Jason Van Dyke shot and killed Laquan McDonald, aged 17. The officer was white and the boy was African-American. At least 5 other officers were present. Van Dyke claimed that the boy had a knife out and was charging at him which justified his shooting the boy. The other officers supported Van Dyke's story.

The city had a dash-board video of the entire event, but did not release it for over a year. The public was very upset by the delay and called for the resignations of Mayor Rahm Emanuel and others. When the video was finally released, the stories of the officers were shown to be very false and not all what the video showed. The culture of the police department came to be seen as lacking value in truthfulness and holding a disregard for justice. (*New York Times, December 6, 2015)*

On December 7, 2015 the *NY Times* reported the "Justice to investigate Chicago police force." One paragraph by Monica Davey and Mitch Smith was very descriptive. "The video outraged many. Yet along with anger over the shooting itself, there is an added element fulling frustration in Chicago: a lingering sense that the authorities from the police department to City Hall, tried to keep the case out of the spotlight as long as possible."

A December 31, 2015 AP article by Sara Burnett and Michael Tarm was headlined, "Chicago police reform focuses on use of force. Mayor announces training changes, expanded Taser use." The next day the *NY Times* reporters wrote that the

FBI had been asked to probe latest police shooting (January 1, 2016).

Then on August 17, 2016, *USA Today's* major story was headlined, "7 cop firings recommended in teen's death." Doug Stanglin wrote that 5 of the officers whose false reporting had been so wrong from the facts of the video were being recommended for dismissal from the force. Officer Van Dyke is being charged with first-degree murder. This story has hearings and trial yet to go BUT this is one of the first steps toward major actions being taken against individual police for their actions while on duty.

While none of these actions will bring back the young man who was killed, the actions do provide a sense of trust in the Justice System ---a level of trust that has been so missing over these past few years. Will it spread to other locations?

Shootings By Police: Two Stories Shared

The *Washington Post* story was headlined: "Cities' diverging strategies—and aftermaths." Its sub-headline was: "Why did Charlotte erupt while Tulsa didn't Police response might play a role." No individual author was given but the story appeared in the September 25, 2016 on page 16A of the *Omaha World-Herald.* Please join by reading these first four paragraphs as given.

"By now it has become almost routine: the police shooting, the outrage, the protests, And the decisions by authorities."

"Do you release the video footage? Do you deploy riot gear? Do you call in the National Guard?"

"For city leaders across the country, this is their new reality in which a tragically uncommon incident—the shooting of a black man by police—has the potential to unleash chaos upon their communities, in which the wrong emotion-can set a city afire."

"Last week it was Charlotte, North Carolina's turn to struggle through those decisions. As it did, Mayor Jennifer Roberts and her police chief were drawing on the painful lessons learned in Ferguson, Missouri, Baton Rouge, Louisiana, Baltimore, Chicago, and Minneapolis."

But in Charlotte the major decisions were centered on "how transparent authorities should be about their investigation" into the death of Keith Lamont Scott. His family and police have given "starkly different accounts of the shooting. Relatives say he was holding a book. Police say he was holding a gun."

Eventually the video footage was released but by then much damage had been done to the main part of the city. Mayor of New Orleans Mitch Landrieu gave this advice, "What we've seen is the faster you release that kind of information and the more the public knows about it, more often than not, it's better."

The stark contrast presented in this story came from the Tulsa, Oklahoma setting. They "waited just two days to release multiple videos and recordings documenting the fatal shooting of a 40-year-old black man in that city on September 16, 2016."

"Tulsa Mayor Dewey Bartlett was also on message: It was something we talked about over the years, that if something of this magnitude were to happen, being transparent, giving out information as quickly and as complete as possible."

The two locations AND the decision to charge the police woman who fired the fatal gun were both decisive and key to the reaction of trust of the people in Tulsa. Strangely, just about two years earlier, Charlotte had gone through a very similar situation and had responded much as Tulsa just did. What was different? Everything according to many!

Conclusion for now

Different cities with very different reactions to very similar events. The directions our justice system needs to take seems to be very obvious as quickness of response, full and quick sharing of all relevant data to the public, and prompt decisions about the right and wrong of the individual cases is the message being sent to us all.

CHAPTER 4

Prosecutors: A Key in the Judicial System

Prosecutors, these judicial leaders in our system of justice have been called by many names. Some of them are even printable! But their actual titles are extremely varied and not at all uniform across the nation. Wikipedia provides the following titles:

> "The titles of prosecutors in state courts vary from state to state and include City Attorney (in MO), Commonwealth's Attorney (in KY and VA), County Attorney (in AZ), County Prosecutor (in NJ), District Attorney (in NC, GA, MA, NY, PA, OK, & TX), District Attorney General (in TN), Prosecuting Attorney (in HA, ID, OH, MI, WA, and WV), State's Attorney (in CT, FL, IL, MD, and VT), State Prosecutor, Attorney General (in DL, and RI), Solicitor (in SC). …most often chosen through local elections…(and the winner) hires other

> attorneys as deputies or assistant to conduct most of the actual work of the office." Note: Example of variation—OH = Prosecuting Attorney but the press always refers to him as Attorney General.

These elected judicial leaders are required by both state and federal laws to follow certain rules such as they must disclose key evidence to the defense (Brady v Maryland, 2013). They are also responsible for deciding which, if any, charges to make in a case. They are usually a lawyer, and subject to potential charges of misconduct. But the American Bar Association has also established a very specific document entitled, Criminal Justice Section Standards Prosecution Function.

The document opens with Part I GENERAL STANDARDS and leads with Standard 3- 1.1 The Function of the Standards. For this book's purpose some words are emphasized to stress clarity for the reader. "These standards are intended to be used as a guide to professional conduct and performance. They are not intended to be used as a criteria for the judicial evaluation of alleged misconduct of the prosecutor to determine the validity of a conviction. They may or may not be relevant in such judicial evaluation, depending upon all the circumstances."

The document continues for 17 pages covering such significant elements of the role and function of a prosecutor. The following very partial list of Standards serve as examples of the complexity of this judicial role.

Conflicts of Interest
Duty to Respond to Misconduct
Special Assistants, Investigative Resources, Experts
Training Programs
Relations with Police
Prompt Disposition of Criminal Cases
Supercession and Substitution of Prosecutor
Investigative Function
Relations with Victims and Prospective Witnesses and Expert Witnesses
Decision to Charge
Relations with Grand Jury
Disclosure of Evidence by the Prosecutor
Plea Discussions
Selection of Jurors Relations with Jury
Role in Sentencing Information Relevant to Sentencing

Even just a quick read of this sample from the total list brings to light numerous qualities and duties of the prosecutor which are subject to major concerns regarding the provision of full justice for all. Examples include Relations with Police which promote or distort full transformation of all data. Selection of jurors who honestly represent "a jury of peers" is another major area of contention. The position is very important and how it is done by a prosecutor is crucial.

The turmoil of the past several years of increased media coverage of all aspects of the Judicial System from initial contact by law enforcement to the final (?) disposition of a case has put the Prosecutorial role into the headlines. Issues such as control of evidence from collection to its use in court and timeliness of moving the judicial process forward and the public sharing of the electronic and other elements of a case are all crucial. They directly impact the level of public trust and confidence in the entire process.

Wikipedia's explanation above is very appropriate to help the reader more fully understand this very important part of our Judicial System. "The prosecutor is the chief legal representative of the prosecution in countries with either the common law adversarial system or the civil law inquisitorial system. The prosecution is the legal party responsible for presenting the case in a criminal trial against an individual accused of breaking the law."

Prosecutors are typically lawyers who possess a law degree, and are recognized as legal professionals by the court in which they intend to represent society...They usually only become involved in a criminal case once a suspect has been identified and charges need to be filed. They are typically employed by an office of the government, with safeguards in place to ensure such an office can successfully pursue the prosecution of government officials."

Prosecutors must often work very closely with the local law enforcement system in order to become fully informed about all details of the case that is before them Such elements as details about the arrest, investigations, interviews, and evidence, etc. are very crucial to the decision as to just what charge or charges are appropriate. The Prosecutor's office generally have a very close working relationship with the police system.

Thus when the police are themselves accused of criminal actions even as a part of what they have done as an officer, the local prosecutor is in a very difficult situation. One of the major suggestions for Judicial Reform is to have a quick method for turning over such a new case to an outside person to function as that case's prosecutor. When President Trump was being investigated for possible illegal Russian influence in his election, the Attorney General Sessions **recused** himself from any role in that investigation.

Prosecutors can be given labels when they do not vacate key cases. Titles such as "Prosecutors Who Aim to Kill" have been given, for example, to five men one of whom is still in office. The "famous-five" prosecutors were identified as follows: Joe Freeman Britt in North Carolina, Robert Macy in Oklahoma, Donnie Myers in South Carolina, Lynne Abraham in Philadelphia, and Johnny Holmes in Texas. Mr. Myers is still in office as of 2016.

"In 2002, a federal appeals court said that Mr. Macy's persistent misconduct 'without doubt harmed the reputation of Oklahoma's criminal justice system,'" the editorial concluded. They closed their analysis as follows: "The rate of death sentences has less to do with the crimes of the people being prosecuted than with the men and women doing the prosecuting."

If reform is to take place, one of the key elements must be selecting stronger and conscientious attorneys with high ethical and moral standards. That will only take place if those who are elected are well-respected by all segments of that governing district.

Some Good News

On August 12, 2016 the Center for Court Innovation (www.courtinnovation.org) posted one of its recommendations for this element of the Judicial System. **Community Prosecution** was described/explained as follows:

"Community prosecution is founded on the idea that prosecutors have a responsibility not only to prosecute cases but to solve public safety problems, prevent crime and improve public confidence in the justice system. Around the country, prosecutors are taking on new responsibilities that reflect this shift— working out of neighborhood offices and collaborating with others (including residents, community groups, and other government agencies) in the development of problem-solving initiatives. In many cases, community stakeholders actually help to set the crime-fighting agenda and participate in the solutions.

Definitions of success are changing as well. Rather than tallying cases won or jail sentences imposed, community prosecutors are measuring the effect of their work on neighborhood quality of life, community attitudes and crime. Working with local prosecutors and national experts such as the Association for Prosecuting Attorneys, the Center for Court Innovation provide

> prosecutor Robert Murray did was produce a transcript of the defendant's interrogation <u>to which Murray had added a false confession</u>."

"Murray admitted falsifying the transcript…When the trial judge found out, charges against the defendant were dismissed." When the state Attorney General appealed the case because the defendant wasn't subjected to any physical brutality, but lost that appeal. "Murray has suffered no punishment, (but) the California State Bar is seeking to suspend him." "…prosecutors are also immune from civil suit, under a Supreme Court-created doctrine called 'absolute immunity.' But if we care about seeing the law enforced fairly and honestly, we need more accountability."

Tamir Rice was killed by a white police officer in Cleveland, OH. The twelve-year old African-American was playing alone in a park in November, 2014 and had a toy gun with him. The video shows the police car arriving across the yard near a gazebo, stopping with the white police shouting for him to put down his gun. Two-seconds later, Tamir was shot and then died.

An Associated Press story printed on December 31, 2015 headline read, "Rice prosecutors felt conviction impossible… Video allegedly shows the Cleveland boy drawing gun." Rice's family and many others have been very upset ever since. Prosecutor Tim McGinty defended his decisions, "We knew that ethically there couldn't be a trial in this case."

McGinty's position was up for election in November, 2016 with the primary in the Spring. An Associated Press story in the Dayton Daily News on March 19, 2016 after the primary led with the headline, "Black voters help oust prosecutor…McGinty critized for handling of Tamir Rice case." ELECTIONS once again show that citizens have the ability to make their voices heard. Since no Republican was running for this position, as of January, 2017 there will be a new County Prosecutor for Cuyahoga County Ohio.

The Standards for Prosecutors cannot be used to remove them from office, but the actions a prosecutor took to not charge the police officer because of the gun—real or not—in the boy's hand would not result in a clear-cut case in court were overturned in the election. The job of a prosecutor is very much still in the public view. His view that he could not convene a jury who could find the police guilty of Tamir's death to be criminal could also be correct. The job is not easy!

Death Penalty Prosecutors

Jordan Smith's June 15, 2016 posting via theintercept. com raised the significant question, "Will the Supreme Court Crack Down on Louisiana's Rogue Prosecutors?" Smith cites author Alex Kozinski who has called an 'epidemic' of prosecutorial misconduct, "the withholding of evidence that might exonerate or mitigate the guilt of a defendant. Failure to turn it over, according to the court's seminal 1963 decision Brady v. Maryland, is a violation of due process.

The University of Michigan Law School's National Registry of Exonerations, 933 of the nearly 1,800 exonerations to date involve official misconduct by prosecutors, police, or other government officials. Thirty-five of those exonerations come from the state of Louisiana alone, where prosecutors have a dismal record of complying with their legal obligations."

Just two weeks later (6-30-2016) Smith's posting summarized his analysis of the problem with these title words, "The Death Penalty is Largely Driven by a Small Number of Overzealous Prosecutors." He cites the Harvard Law School's Fair Punishment Project and its recent report that identifies "the small club of five so-called deadliest prosecutors."

Smith then added, "Together, the five prosecutors, only one of whom is still in office, secured 440 capital convictions—the equivalent of 15 percent of the nation's current death row population." In July 1976, the U.S. Supreme Court decision in *Gregg v. Georgia* reauthorized the use of capital punishment ushering in the modern death penalty era.

Our society must now be able to make decisions about prosecutors that have rarely in the past been based on such choices as the penalties they advocate. Doing just this may be a vital step in this element of Justice For All.

CHAPTER 5

Leaders of Law Enforcement: Sheriffs, Chiefs, and Commisioners

Nearly every law enforcement agency has a designated leader. Those in such leadership positions may be elected (county sheriffs), or appointed by local government bodies such as local townships, cities, villages, etc. which are also elected. The key point here is that local citizens do have a direct or just one-step removed from a direct 'say-so' in who is to be the top official leader of a local law enforcement agency. Thus elections are vital as shown in the second chapter of this book.

These leaders play a major role in how well a local agency carries out its duties. Is the agency turned into a local fund-raiser for its local community via zero tolerance for minor crimes which thus generates many dollars for the local budget? Or has its hiring and training policies kept it in sync with the actual demographic nature of the people being served? Are its officers own attitudes toward others a part of the screening/hiring process? Are citizen complaints about the actions, attitudes, applications, etc.,given significant attention by the leaders?

Has the leader been a manager or a leader seeking to improve the total organization? Managers simply manage while leaders are working to make the agency fully tied to the needs of their community. This type of law enforcement is essential to meet the goal of "Justice for All." Does the leadership commit itself and the agency to the full support of the Constitution of the nation and the laws of its elected people? Their typical oath of allegiance says they do, but do they take that obligation seriously?

A number of major investigations by the federal authorities such as the Department of Justice have resulted in major changes that the questions above have been seriously addressed. In other studies the results have been highly negative but have identified very specific actions that need to be taken by the local agency-be it a county or a city/township/village.

However, there are many locations and leaders of law enforcement whose own allegiance to the U.S. Constitution and laws is much in doubt. Some even proudly boast about their belief that they are above the Constitution. They, on their own, will decide which laws and parts of the Constitution they will enforce and follow in their work.

One such county sheriff in Arizona was in 2016 dis-elected after years of being able to assert that he would decide which laws passed by congress or others would apply to his populous county. Wikipedia's full story provides key details. Maricopa County (AZ) Sherriff Joe

Arpaio and his County Attorney Thomas had cost taxpayers $8,670,110 dollars to settle 11 cases brought against them. In addition "As of June 2014, costs to Maricopa County taxpayers related to Arpaio's and Thomas's failed corruption investigations exceeded $44 million, not including stafftime." Of course, our newly elected President on August 25, 2017 pardoned him for his legal issues after he had been convicted but before he had been sentenced. He was in his mid-eighties by then.

The Southern Poverty Law Center (SPLC) has been following our nation's laws and practices for decades. Among its most recent area of focus has been an organization of county and other law enforcement leaders called the **Constitutional Sheriffs and Peace Officers Association** (CSPOA. This organization claims to have the support of 400 Sheriffs and 5,000 members across the country.

SPLC Intelligence Report (Summer 2016}

The cover 'headline+' of this Report reads, "Line in the Sand. Constitutional Sheriffs' Movement Proposing Defiance of Government,Spreading in Rural America." Inside the Report summarizes its work as follows: "A radical movement of 'constitutional sheriffs' has been growing since the 2009 formation of the CSPOA. A survey of sheriffs shows that the movement, which pushes plainly UNconstutional claims that the officers can defy the government and decide which laws they will enforce, is exploiting issues like gun, environmental and land use regulations with real success."

The Report by Mark Potok and Ryan Lenz illustrates the belief and thought process of this organization. "The group (CSPOA) says it is part of a 'growing movement of public officials who are drawing a line in the sand by interposing themselves between the sometimes over reaching Federal Government and your constitutionally guaranteed rights.'" It then claims that local county sheriffs can stop outside law enforcement officials from enforcing laws they (CSPOA) deem unconstitutional. The sheriff, it says, is the highest elected official in the county and has the authority to stop this insanity.

It seems very clear to the vast majority of local law enforcement officials and those who work as an integral part of the basic system of our local, state, and federal system of government that this belief system is highly inconsistent with our Justice System. The problem is very clear. Such power grabbing actions they propose as being "Just" is a direct attack on our democratic system and its Constitutional system.

Given that our system of justice has not always worked in concert with the goals of the nation, but it has always kept the 'power' in the hands of the people via the election system.

With organizations such as the SPLC helping via their regular studies and watchdog efforts on our nation's behalf, the country has been able to make corrections.

Chris Hoffman, the sheriff of Raville County, Mont., told those making this study that he does sympathize with his constituents' anger at environmental land us and at gun use. But he added, "The United States is a nation of laws and sheriffs need to help restore tranquility... But if we're not part of the solution toward calming those fears and getting those people calmed down, then we're part ofthe problem." I agree strongly! He makes sense!

In a letter from SPLC founder Morris Dees, he expresses his trust in these words. "I know that most officers---including tens of thousands who will read this issue---will also be appalled. We're doing everything we can to expose this threat to the rule of law." This book is a part of that larger effort in support of the rule of law.

Milwaukee Police Chief

The rioting, looting, burning, and general violence that came to a portion of Milwaukee following another police killing of the Black young man (Sylville K. Smith) was seen by millions via TV. The Chief of the Police Department, Edward Flynn, made himself very available to the press as he tried to provide some key details. He stressed that the situation was still being investigated and the autopsy results were not yet available. This is a local Police Chief who is taking an active role in bringing about changes in his own city.

The Associated Press (August 15, 2016) by Grechen Ehlke and Todd Richmond wrote that Flynn said,.." that based on the silent video from the unidentified officer's body camera, he certainly appeared to be within lawful bounds." Chief Flynn also said that the officer was Black. The entire episode from the start of the traffic stop until shots were fired took only about 25 seconds.

The story continued, "He (Flynn) said Smith ran about a few dozen feet and turned toward the officer while holding a gun... lt was in his hand. He was raising up with it." The violence was so quick to take place and that was a problem. It grew out of a long history of problems between the police and the 4 out 10 citizens who are Black.

The next day, a Sunday, about 3 dozen citizens were out with trash bags to help clean up the devastated area. One volunteer picked up a bullet casing and handed it to a police man. "Darlene Rose, 31, said that she understands the anger that fueled the violence, but it doesn't help. I feel like if you're going to make a difference, it's got to be an organized difference. The people that came and looted, we're not going to see them here today." A citizen joins with him in a public way.

The resistant on the police side has been matched by a restraint among community leaders, who have not blamed the police but said the upheaval is the product of deeper inequalities that have led to Wisconsin having the highest incarceration rate for African American men in the United States. This from the *Christian Science Monitor* of August 29, 2016.

Shawn Alexander, an African-American professor at University of Kansas, stated, "That focus on deeper issues matches a similar shift in the broader 'Black Lives Matter' movement which earlier this month released a platform of policy demands that *go* far beyond protests against police brutality." Chief Flynn, fully agrees. He has asked for Federal help and has pledged his full cooperation. He knows that the investigation will provide the city with major targets for improvement and he looks forward to doing his best to meeting them.

David Brown: Chief of Dallas Police

Given the major problem of the loss of five policemen in Dallas, their Chief of Police has been much in the news ever since. A native of Dallas, he has a special interest in making his own city a shining example of good policing. The tragic element in the loss of five men to a single shooter was that those same five and dozens of others had just been walking with hundreds of protestors upset with the shootings by police officers in Minneapolis and Baton Rouge.

Talking and walking with the protestors and pausing to take "selfies" with them gave proof to the theory that having made a major change in policing can make a difference. Then the shooting took place and once again, Dallas was in the nation's focus.

Chief Brown, a black man, had moved the force forward charting a new course for the Dallas Police Department. It took real courage as the Police Union has not been pleased with at least parts of the newness! But Dallas Mayor Mike Rawlins credits the departments training in conflict resolution techniques far before other cities did the same as being a key factor. Brown is a native of Dallas and has risen within the police department to this position. He has experienced justice as a minority and translated that to his leadership activities.

Mayor Rawlins said, "We are one of the premier community policing cities in the country. And this year, we have the fewest police-officer-related shootings than any large city in America." He went on, "So we are working hard to improve and there's always room for improvement. But we are the best in our class."

The Community Policing he was talking about has been described as fostering "proactive interaction between officers and residents." It seeks to build better understandings, improve human interactions, and develop much increased trusting. When asked why Dallas still did not have as many minority members as it wanted, the Chief quickly responded, "We are trying to hire right now! Come on down---the application center is open!"

News reports a week or two later indicated that many new applicants had heard his messages. Young men and women liked what they were hearing about his department. They wanted much to be a part of it with him in charge. This would help them be a part of a dynamic new force within America's law enforcement system. They would be a part of the dynamic move within our nation to bring about more openness in our justice system.

Police Unions Impede Justice

"When Police Unions Impede Justice" was the headline for the *New York Times* editorial on Sunday, September 4, 2016. Across the nation municipal governments have signed contracts with their own local police associations giving them much power over their own members. These contracts have shielded the members from major complaints from citizens over their "punishment for brutalized behavior."

Chicago is the most recent example of a lengthy discrimination over the case of 17year old Laqauan McDonald who was shot by a police officer nearly two years ago. The police at the scene testified that the boy was running toward the officer and carrying a knife. Film of the incident showed that he was, instead, running away from the shooter and not carrying a knife. Misleading prosecution or actual lying seemed evident.

The TIMES editorial continued, "But it was not until last month that the city's inspector general recommended firing several officers, some of whom have since retired, for making false statements." Mr. Eddie Johnson has now made administrative charges against the officers which could lead to their being fired. "It is incredible that this is the first official disciplinary action taken against the officers, 22 months after the killing." And if the Board votes to dismiss them, the officers will be able to challenge the action in court.

The editorial closes with these fighting words, "To restore public confidence in the law, elected officials around the country will have to stop reflexively trucking to police unions and demand contracts that actually reflect the public interest." The movement will be a major one and one to be watched very closely.

Ohio Supreme Court reverses ruling in local case

The case involved the use of juvenile convictions in an adult's sentence. "Prior juvenile convictions can't be used to enhance the sentence of an adult, a split Ohio Supreme Court ruled Thursday reversing a lower court decision in a Montgomery County case." The ruling went on by a split 4-3 decision, "that an adult's prison term based on juvenile adjudications violated both state and federal constitutions."

There was much focus on the fact that a juvenile adjudication does not provide a right to a jury trial, it cannot be used to increase the sentence for an adult in the case. The Supreme Court remanded the case to the trial court for re-sentencing. When juvenile records are sealed they must remain closed and not resurrected to be used again later for that individual.

A Conviction Overturned

"More than 9 years after Brenden Dassey was sent to prison for the murder of Teresa Halbach, a judge rules his confession was 'involuntary' and his lawyer 'indefensible.' Will he go free?" This leading headline in the *People,* August 8, 2016 magazine story by Chris Harris,the young man, now 26, has "a reason to hope he may soon be released. On August 12, 2016, U.S. Magistrate Judge William E. Duffin overturned Dassey's murder conviction stating that his confession had been 'involuntary' and that the 'misconduct' of his defense attorney Len Kachinsky was 'indefensible.'"

Dassey's statements to police "*were* completely contradicted by the lack of physical evidence." Judge Duffin ruled that Dassey's "age, intellectual deficits and the absence of a supportive adult at his interrogation discounted the confession." The case once again brings to the surface that society must be prepared to retry or forget many old cases on the books. When such major errors have been made in these previous cases,the old adages about just letting the past be the past are no longer current. You need to retry this case from its own beginning.

Local Ohio Case

The major front page headline (September 16, 2016) in the Dayton Daily News read: "Sheriff says records stolen in federal suit. Woman says she was pepper-sprayed while restrained at jail." Mark Gokavi, staff writer wrote: "Montgomery County Sheriff Phil Plummer is investigating what he called an 'orchestrated' inside job to steal or destroy records at the center of a federal lawsuit brought by a Brookville woman (Amber Swink) who was pepper sprayed while restrained at the county jail." No official film was ever found, but a copy did surface for the public.

The case and its missing records now seems to have been instrumental in the promotion of the Sgt. Judith Sealey to a Captain position. "The sheriff pointed out that incident place in November, 2015. Sealey was promoted in January, 2016, he was made aware of the incident in March, 2016, and that he just saw the video on Wednesday." That there was a coverup is clear because the video was totally missing in the filing system. Sealey is African-American and this may have been a complicating factor.

Sheriff Plummer said, "Sealey's use of force report,the log of when jail employees checked on Swink in the harness chair and the video are missing." The sheriff continued, "The month before, the month after is all the way it should be... (November is) gone. So to me, that says somebody deleted it and tampered with it. We've got to get that forensically looked at."

It does seem that some staff within the County Jail acted to prevent the Sherriff from being knowledgeable about this case prior to his approval of her promotion to Captain. Who did what when has not been determined, but the prisoner, Amber Swink is now out of jail and has been awarded a $375,000 settlement for the jail's actions Wikipdia reports. Sherriff Plummer is a rare republican office holder among mostly democratic officers in that county government. I had voted for him a number of times over the years.

Conclusion

Local situations of all types occur throughout our nation involving local law enforcement leaders. Too many are still of unconstitutional and illegal nature and need to be changed. Too many result in millions of dollars of tax money being paid to wronged prisoners as a result. Whether one is politically conservative or liberal, **this situation is unlawful** and must also be changed. Such changes will result in an improved **Justice for All** system.

CHAPTER 6

Juvenile Justice System

The system by which juveniles are brought before the court for justice are varied and do not always follow the same system for adults. They are established and based upon known factors in justice and in how best to treat a youthful offender. While some courts are found to be very appropriate for children under a certain *age,* other courts in the same jurisdiction are woefully inadequate. Juvenile Justice is not the same as that provided for adults and its differences are very significant and must be understood by society as well as by those in the legal and judicial system.

The Montgomery County Ohio has a system for dealing with juvenile offenders in a very positive way. It holds fast to first trying a child in its own system and with its own judges and participating judges. It uses its own Child Advocates known as Court Appointed Special Advocates (CASA) each of whom has been well-trained. I served as a CASA for about a ten year period.   Each CASA becomes an official Officer of the Court and as such, can attend all appropriate school meetings, read all mental and school tests, and interview all persons related to the child's case.

This county also has a Drug Court which is used for those youth who have incurred drug or alcohol abuse charges. These youth spend about a year of time as they continue school and take drug treatment programs. Their program leads them to a high school graduation with a full ceremony and key parents and others available. The 'graduates' have a recidivist rate now over many years of less than 10%--far below the much higher rate of return to more convictions.

SPLC Study Calls Attention

The Southern Poverty Law Center (SPLC) study report highlighted needless prosecution of children as adults in New Orleans. The report presented solid data about the large number of children being sent to adult courts even though major research evidence about child development has shown this to be very inappropriate. The practice is now under study in New Orleans, but now also throughout that state and the nation.

Given that the age limit in Louisiana is only 17 and that many youth of that level of development are now moved onto the adult court level. The NY Times of May 8, 2016 headline *read, "Louisiana May Raise Agefor Juvenile Defendants."* Then just a week later on May 15,2016 its own lead story by Eric Eckholm in the National Section was headlined, *"Moving Away From Treating 17-Year Old Offenders as Adults"* with the sub-head: *"Raise the Age Push Has States Considering*

Justice System Changes. Such headlines are indicative of major movement among our states.

Changes in our U.S. System of Justice are underway already. Wins in court cases, reports which identify problems, and public opinions are making a difference. But the need for major reforms continues. It is good to know that there are groups such as the SPLC and *The New York Times* that are working actively to bring such reforms into reality. Such help is essential if such changes are to be made permanent.

Prison Legal News

The May 2016 issue of this magazine carried the headline, *"Lawsuit Claims Florida Teen Raped, Beaten in Prison Initiation Ritual."* The article then proceeded to explain that the Florida's Correctional Facilities for youthful offenders are often a part of the state's adult prison system. Therefore Florida incarcerates more minors than any other state in the nation. About 140 juveniles are housed in detention centers on any given day, and in July 2013 that included a 17- year-old known only as "R.W."

"According to a lawsuit filed on January 17, 2016 by the Southern Poverty Law Center (SPLC) and Florida Institutional Legal Services,Therefore Sumter Correctional Institution Guard Bruce A. Kiser, Jr. stood by and watched while at least six youth beat and sexually assaulted R.W. in a bathroom in F Dorm as part of a prison initiation rite called a 'test of heart.'"

R.W. was cut "repeatedly with sharpened pieces of barbed wire, choked unconscious and raped with a broom-stick on July 24, 2013. Kiser never reported the incident." Look at "R.W. v. Kiser, U.S.D.C., (M.D. Fla.) Case 5: 16-cv-00045-WTH-PRL."

"An investigation by the FDOC's Office of the Inspector General noted Kiser's inaction...but Kiser reportedly was not disciplined for his role in the attack and continues to be employed as a prison guard." The FDOC had previously settled a similar lawsuit and agreed to pay $700,000 to a youth who had been permanently injured during a 'test-of-heart' at the Lancaster Correctional Institution. Still another juvenile died in 2014 from injuries in a very similar incident at a Florida prison aimed at serving youthful offenders.

Such blatantly illegal actions must be stopped immediately in order to protect juvenile offenders. To ignore their taking place puts an entire system of healthy imprisonment and cooperative return into society at risk.

School to Prison Pipeline

The Spring 2013 issue of the SPLC quarterly magazine, *Teaching Tolerance,* devoted its cover story to this very issue. It is lengthy because it includes numerous statements from those most affected by the various programs. I will only try to highlight the full story and to use those extensive quotes sparingly, BUT I do urge all readers to consider this chapter as one of the most important to the total topic of reform of our system of justice.

"In Meridian, Miss. Police regularly arrest and transport youths to a juvenile detention center for minor classroom misbehaviors. In Jefferson Parish, La., according to a U.S.

Department of Justice complaint, school officials have given armed police 'unfettered authority to stop, frisk, detain, question, search, and arrest school children on and off school grounds."

In Birmingham, Ala., police officers are permanently stationed in nearly every high school."

In fact, the above citations only scratch the surface of the nationwide extent of this problem in our schools. Hundreds of school districts employ similar policies that push students out of the classroom and into the criminal justice system at alarming rates. I could only present a few of many clippings thus far collected about the "school-to-prison-pipeline."

"Last month, (Spring 2013), Sen. Richard Durban,D-111., held the first federal hearing on the school-to-prison-pipeline-an important step toward ending policies that favor incarceration over education and disproportionately push minority students and students with disabilities out of schools and into jails."

Many schools now have policies which include a police present in the school buildings and even in school classrooms. *Teacher control of their own classrooms has too often been given over to the police who can use their force on selected students.* When teachers can opt to turn over a problem to a member of the police, the problem is enlarged dramatically. Students are too often pushed out of the classroom into a variety of other punishments. They are then much more likely to be introduced into the criminal justice system.

Who is in this system? "Students from two groups-racial minorities and children with disabilities-are disproportionally represented in the school-to-prison pipeline. African American students, for instance, are 3-5 times more likely than their white classmates to be suspended or expelled...Black children constitute 18 percent of students but they account for 46 percent of those suspended more than *once.*"

For students with disabilities, the numbers are equally disturbing. One study reported that "while 8.6 percent of public school children have been identified as having disabilities that affect their ability to learn, these students make up 32 percent of youth in juvenile detention centers." The problems involved with these cases only grow over time. Samples of recent articles merely document this problem is growing.

Solutions to These School Problems

Your local paper illustrates some of the solutions. From the Dayton Daily News comes this story. The Dayton City Commission has voted to put a change on the ballot. They want to earmark a significant change that would bring 25% of their local income tax back into the city coffers.

Those dollars would be designated for early childhood education for Dayton's youth. Their goal is to reach out to these youngest by making vast improvements in their early learning.

A quality early life experience would also tie into improved nutrition. The headline of the January 12, 2016 article read, "Preschool ideal time to focus on kids healthy eating habits," and it subline read, "Study says its (sic) good to start kids on healthy lifestyles at ages 3-5." If this passes in November, the result will be a very strong start to bringing the Dayton

City Schools into a growth atmosphere. Good food and good eating are both tied to better learning.

The *Christian Science Monitor* September 7, 2015 headline read, "Better handling of juveniles in court: Justice reformers press for much reduced use of physical force." For well more than a decade a growing number of juvenile justice reformers have been arguing against the misuse of all types of force. "... routine use of shackling of juveniles including the use of other forms of physical restraint. They say the automatic use of restraints is not in line with the rehabilitative purpose of the juvenile courts and that it limits youths' ability to participate in helpful groups and experiences. One team has begun to work directly with schools... "to try to reduce school-based arrests, their defense, tends to hurt and humiliate them, and in some cases, traumatizes them." Less of such negative side-effects is the real and helpful goal.

"In the five years after Miami *ended* automatic shackling, 20.000 youths freely appeared in court without incident!" This was the answer and proof for those who wanted to be able to stay with the old method according to Stacy Teicher Khandaroo, staff writer for the CSM. The hope is for the slight change to be used in more courts very soon.

The same author (STK) wrote the cover story for the 2-16-2015 issue of CSM, *"Keeping kids from crime: How an alternative to lockups-a 'continuum of care'-is changing juvenile justice."* This lengthy article follows several young men through their time with juvenile justice in Lucas County Ohio.

"Treyvon's case is emblematic of a quiet revolution in juvenile justice sweeping across the country...Localities are launching initiatives to provide counseling, drug treatment, and other support for young offenders rather than locking them up." One innovation borrowed from Portland, Ore., is the "new Lucas County Youth Assessment Center-a place where police can bring kids directly to determine what should be done with them." Jail would be a much later choice in the minds of the police and possibly would become a never experience.

A key part of the Centers' goal is to reduce the number of African-Americans in the system. While they come from 22 percent people of color, they made up 71percent of all those admitted to the secure juvenile detention in 2013. "The average detention population went down 45 percent from 2009 to 2013, but for youth of color it went down 64 percent." which many critics say, create new trends to *reduce* a 'pipeline' to prison which is mostly for minorities." Another positive change to reduce juvenile detention and recidivism for sure.

Still Other Solutions

The *New York Times* editorial of May 22, 2016 admonished all local residents with the headline, "New York Teenagers Dumped in Adult Jails." The editorial then went on to remind all New Yorkers that the Supreme Court has said clearly that it finds it to be morally and constitutionally wrong to equate offenses committed by 17 year olds to be the same as those carried out by adults. One new bill has already passed the Senate in New York and the House needs to do the same. "Change in New York is long overdue," was how they closed this editorial and I fully agree.

Another *New York Times* (September 11, 2016) editorial entitled, "Juvenile Sentences That Defy the Law," this time wondered "Why are Michigan's prosecutors ignoring the Supreme Court?" It then went on to say that throughout the state Michigan courts are just flouting two recent decisions. The first ruling, in 2012, banned mandatory life-without parole sentences for juveniles in homicide cases. While it did make an exception for especially horrendous cases, the thrust was to eliminate this sentence.

Then in January, 2016 the Justices clarified that this new rule was also retroactive and applied to all such cases from the past-about 2300 persons nationwide. But in Michigan with 363 such cases, prosecutors seem to be convinced that most need to remain in the "life without-parole" situation. Two prosecutors seem to be convinced that they should not move to give any current detainees even a slight break.

"It's hard to imagine that a prosecutor would blithely seek life sentences again. Now it is up to federal judges to force Michigan's misbehaving prosecutors to follow the law." The initiative is now up to the local courts to begin to enforce what the Supreme Court has made the law of our land.

The *Christian Science Monitor's* lead author for stories about the juvenile courts, Stacy Teicher Khadaroo, is still at work. Her September 19, 2016 article summed up her story. It read "Fighting truancy: one caring person: Children come to school when they know someone cares if they're there, research shows." In the front page of this story is this revealing short article. "WHY IT MATIERS: When students miss 10 percent of school, it lowers the likelihood of them learning to read by third grade. For high schoolers, chronic absenteeism in even one year results in at least a five-fold increase in the likelihood of them dropping out."

Well within the article is this key quote by Manny Aponte, Gilbert Stuart Middle School in Providence, RI talking about his mentor, Justin Roias. "He motivates me… I have no other people like him...that's always on me, pushing *me.*" By the end of last school year, one line in the story told the real message. "By June, the number of Gilbert Stuart sixth-graders who were chronically absent had been cut in half."

Concerns About Knowledge Gained

"As Graduation Rates Rise, a Fear Diplomas Fall Short: Experts Question Whether Standards Meet the Needs of Colleges and Careers." were the two headlines on the article by Motoko Rich in *The New York Times* page one article on December 27, 2015. Just as one major story makes it to the front page of a major newspaper, the headliners are given a possible glitch in the story. When more students are now graduating, instead of celebrating, the nay-sayers are quickly there to raise questions.

In Dayton,OH a lead article by Julie Carr Smith of the Associated Press called for "Charter evaluation rules updated: The new framework applies to the 2015-2016 sponsor evaluations which will include academic data from the current school year." While this encouraging news appeared on December 28, 2015, the "new" item was, "Sponsors held to same standards as public schools." Many agree!

Another element to look at is the FREE vouchers given to children whose parents can decide to spend them at any place in Ohio. The Monday, July 15, 2016 article in the Dayton Daily News carried the sad news, "Education: Voucher users lag peers on state tests; Study looks at Ohio students who used EdChoice program." The Foredam Institute who created the study has been a Voucher-choice advocate and was surprised at the results. The problem is real and needs to be followed and corrected when found.

"Ohio students who attended private schools thanks to vouchers performed worse on state tests than comparable students who remained in struggling public schools." The issue may have been caused by the ever-changing "state testing program" but the results were still troubling. The results of the new testing were just made available on September 16, 2016 but those results are not yet available. Bottom line: nearly every school in the state has had major drops of its scoring.

The Sunday Review of the *New York Times* carried a major article by Paul Tough headlined, "To Help Kids Thrive, Coach Their Parents." Written for the May 22. 2016 issue, the story's main point was summed up by the separate subhead, "Adults can be taught to create an environment for success." The adults who followed Trough's advice were counseled to play with their children." This would not be so new at all as too many teachers who have been arguing exactly just such intergenerational play for decades. Perhaps these words in a vital section of the Sunday paper will turn the trick. The issue is finding the time for the adults.

Several of my own previous books are much in agreement with this finding. **Summer Children: Ready or Not for School (1986}** strongly emphasized exactly such child-active parent behavior. A second book filled with annotated detailed summaries of over 50 studies from universities, professional associations, local school districts, and leading scholars clearly show how giving a child the time to grow and mature produces much success. Its title was **Real Facts from Real Schools (1995}.**

The January 6, 2016 issue of the *New York Times* carried an opinion piece by Vicki Abeles. Her headline read, "Is School Making Our Children Ill?" Her views become very clear as we read, "Children living in poverty who aspire to college face the same daunting administrative arms race... Even those not bound for college are ground down by the constant measurement in schools under pressure to push through mountains of rote, impersonal material as early as preschool...Modern education is actually making them sick."

An April 24, 2016 article in the *New York Times* focused on "Race and the Testing Wars: More minority parents and teachers are joining the opt-out movement." The writer, Kate Taylor, presents a lot of information about this issue. She concludes by quoting Warren Simmons, a senior fellow at the Annenberg Institute for School Reform in Boston University.

He said, "Test scores can't offer policy makers much guidance in the absence qualitative assessments-of the curriculum, of teacher training, of the support a school is receiving from the district and state." "We don't need another round of tests to tell us that schools are struggling," Simmons concluded!

The testing movement has shown with children having to give up learning time to accommodate more testing time. Teach, not test, is an answer I see becoming more and more current today.

Conclusion

In a private letter to me from the folks at the SPLC, they shared a major achievement from the state of Mississippi. The state closed a very dangerous prison that's been run by private-for-profit firms since 2003. The Walnut Grove Correctional Facility was labeled, "one of the ten worst prisons in America."

Now, some six years after SPLC sued to stop the barbaric treatment of children, some as young as 13, is closing its doors. "Youthful offenders at Walnut Grove endured rampant violence and sexual assaults, often by the guards who were paid to protect them. One young man suffered severe brain damage after he was stabbed and beaten during a fight that was facilitated by a guard."

"The U.S. Justice Department investigators reported that sexual abuse at Walnut Grove-including brazen sexual misconduct by prison staffers-was among the worst that we have seen in any facility anywhere in the nation." After several more years of legal maneuvering the final closing was ordered by a federal judge. "The bottom line is that it doesn't pay to put criminal justice in the hands of profiteers. We hope that all states and the Department of Homeland Security will shut down the private prisons for good." I am proud to have been a SPLC member for well over 20 years!"

Gary Gately's summary of the MacArthur Foundation report on Juvenile Justice in this January 5, 2015 article is very complete. He included these four key bullets under the heading "The report recommended:

- Transfer of youths to the adult system should never be automatic, and judges, not prosecutors, should decide when it's appropriate to transfer a case.
- Adult sentencing standards, including life without parole, should never be applied to juveniles.
- Adolescents should not be placed in adult jails or prisons. Holding them with adults can actually make youths more likely to commit new crimes.
- If youth are placed in adult facilities, provisions of the Prison Rape Elimination Act (PREA) should be strictly enforced. Youths under 18 should not be housed with the adult population, adult facilities must maintain separation between adults and youths; and youths must not be subjected to isolation as a way to comply with PREA."

Hopefully juvenile facilities such as found in Dayton and Toledo OH need to provide full mental and physical assessments of all youths brought in by the police. (See Chapter 15) This would provide separate and full care which is so essential prior to any judicial decisions. The numerous suggestions presented in this chapter are essential for an appropriate action to make sure that **Justice for All includes our juveniles.**

CHAPTER 7

Educ. For Prisoners

It seems so obvious to me that providing educational opportunities for inmates while they are still incarcerated would make so much sense. But, the truth is that many places find the system to be MUCH less than cooperative. But let's give it a chance to fly and see how it goes. My knowledge of "in-prison" time for education is limited to one rather short experience. But it was not a good one although I did a lot of observing and collecting data.

For example my minimum-security prison had gradually eliminated almost all kinds of formal education opportunities for its prisoners-most of whom would be most likely to advance in job and social living readiness is just a few years. No college education programs were available and only a few career-apprenticeship programs still existed. All of this lack was in a state with dozens of colleges and schools offering course work for inmates. But our institution limited access to typewriters and computers! Frustrating!

Patrik Johnson's article in the *Christian Science Monitor* on September 7, 2015 was given the headline, "Southern justice, with diplomas." Just above its headline was this: "Prison reform sweeps into America's most conservative corners, led by GOP governors." Also on the front page was this sidebar: "WHY IT MATTERS Georgia has led the way in prison reform in the South. Including $12 million for education. The reforms are part of a broad shift in thinking among conservatives and liberals alike, away from warehousing criminals and toward rehabilitating prisoners."

Jasmiyah Whitehead and 18 other young women achieved a historic achievement in a state originally conceived of to help imprisoned English debtors start a new life graduating from its first high school behind bars. This effort in Georgia was designed to combat a 40 percent recidivism rate "has emerged in part to curb budget-choking costs of nearly three decades of mass incarceration policies."

Georgia had previously landed 1out of every 13 Georgians under some sort of state correctional supervision. The South, as a whole, has been among the highest per capita prison populations. "But a slew of criminal reform laws in Georgia, including a $12 million prison education initiative in the state aimed at giving prisoners skills and motivation to reenter society as law-abiding citizens, has stopped the prison boom and reduced the prison population by 5,000 since 2013."

Georgia Governor Nathan Deal said, "Cost saving is certainly an important [driver of reforms], but most important is saving people's lives." The general philosophy is that if you want to reduce the recidivism rate you should take major advantage of their incarceration rate to give them time to improve their skills. Then when they are ready to leave the prison, you have given them real skills and abilities to sell in the market.

"Six weeks after graduating from the state's first prison welding certificate program, John Turner who had been incarcerated for 13 years, was released...A few days later, Mr. Turner was holding his first paycheck from a welding job. He is now recouping lost time with his son, who is 13...We feel we have an opportunity here and we can't squander it."

Pall Over Arkansas Inmate Program to Fight Blight

Campbell Robertson and Ethan Tate combined to write this August 14, 2016 story for the *New York Times* National edition. The city of Pine Bluff, AR had been declining dramatically over the past decades. It had many long-since abandoned houses that needed to be removed and their land made reusable.

"Starting last fall and scheduled to run for two years, the program was free the economically ailing city of Pine Bluff of 600 blighted houses while the participants here in the state with the nation's fastest growing prison population, were to gain valuable instruction, experience, and even some money." Pine Bluff was to benefit and the men with lots of time on their hands were also to benefit. It looked to be like a 'win-win' type of situation.

But with all of the homes to take down, there was dust--and MORE dust. That meant that there would also be asbestos to be dealt with. "Scant protection for the workers in a municipal project done on the cheap," described the work process over time. The city did get its 600 houses demolished, but the inmates ended up with much less that they had been led to believe.

Such results strongly suggest the real goals were to save money for the local city and to do so by having as little "costly" extras such as appropriate safety equipment and tools for the prison "learners/doers" would need. Not a workable solution for this problem.

Yoga Changing Lives in Prisons

The *Dayton Daily News* of July 30, 2016, carried this headline for a story by Rosemary Ponnekanti of the News Tribune service of Tacoma, WASH. The pre-heading was, "YOGA FOR ALL," and the sub-heading read, "For many, yoga can be a pathway to address trauma." The opening paragraphs tell about this not being a typical yoga class. Instead there are uniforms, noisy fans, locked doors, gray lockers, and institutional carpet.

It is, rather, a class for some women incarcerated at the Washington Corrections Center for Women in Purdy, Wash. Their teacher comes from a group, Yoga Behind Bars-a Seattle based nonprofit. "The results? Hope and peace for offenders, safer prisons and communities and a refocus for yoga itself." One of the students, inmate Candace Ralston describes her own view, "This is a terribly loud, abusive environment. Yoga helps you find peace. It saved me!"

Yoga inside prison walls isn't very new. "Begun informally by a Seattle yoga teacher in 2004,Yoga Behind Bars began giving classes inside the Kind County Juvenile Detention Center in 2007, and has expanded to include several more facilities." The operation has won awards, trained more than 250 teachers and in "February saw 10 men at Stafford Creek graduate as yoga teachers-the first in-prison yoga teacher training in the nation."

A 2007 study of prisoners in North Carolina found that taking four or more yoga classes significantly reduced their recidivism rates to 8.5 percent, compared to national rates of 43 percent. "And decades of studies have shown yoga helps people in general cope better with stress, trauma and physical problems."

Yoga classes were taught as part of the regular curriculum at the Elkton Prison for federal prisoners near Youngstown, OH. These were taught outdoors when possible and brought similar results to the men at this minimum security prison. They, too, have found it to be an excellent recreational setting which gives them a more "centered life." Unfortunately, many of the Bureau of Prisons have been forced to cut all kinds of education programs in recent years.

The Elkton institution had much difficulty in giving education a major place in its program of activities. Any excuse seemed to be appropriate for canceling all education classes just so that all teachers could be used for "emergency" shakedowns or so that all" staff might be able to participate in Staff Appreciation events. Any excuse was good enough, it seemed!

I was a tutor for the General Education program at Elkton. Some of our men were very enthused about the program and gave it much serious attention. I had 3 men who ASKED for more time to be assigned to them for GED so that they could get in more time sooner. This enabled them to make faster progress toward being able to take the exams. Their problem? We could rarely count on having a class for them while I was there because our staff member was often pulled away from us for other duties. And whenever he was gone, the classes for the day were all canceled.

I also was able to provide assistance to a young man of 24 who had already graduated from The Ohio State University with a degree in Mechanical Engineering and was one semester short of a Master Degree in the same field. He wanted to teach a class in basic Physics but he knew so little about how to teach. We worked together on materials and methods for weeks.

I knew so little about physics (1course in high school) but we were able to make good use of our time together.

His class was offered as one of many for the Fall program of classes which carried no credit per se. But the number signing up for Physics reached the room limit and then some. It was a very mixed class ranging from one man with a Ph.D. in Chemistry who just wanted to refresh his knowledge of Physics to a number who just wanted to begin this study. The class went very well and even though I was released from Elkton on November 13, 2015, I have been informed that it was continued in the Spring term. All students did have to have passed their GED program or already had at least a high school diploma in order to be eligible to take any of these classes.

Key Question: Why could these type of courses be worked through one or more of the dozens of colleges nearby to include some type of college credit? How can all prisons-state and federal-be funded and expected to make such recidivism-defeating help available?

New Federal Tool Just Signed

A new federal education tool has just recently been signed-9-22-2016. The President and Congress took an important step toward closing the achievement gap in the nation's schools and stemming the tide of students needlessly pushed out of class and into the school to-prison pipeline. The Every Student Succeeds Act was signed by the President last week. It did not replace the No Child Left Behind law, but it does encourage school districts to take a closer look at their discipline practices.

This is a very significant step because suspensions and expulsions not only push children out of the classroom, they can also be a student's first step toward the juvenile justice system. This law now recognizes this danger. The Southern Poverty Law Center's release to me and others explains the essence the new law.

"It requires school districts to show how they are taking steps to curb discipline practices that remove students from the classroom. This can include identifying schools with high rates of discipline. School districts are also being asked to adopt discipline practices backed by evidence and keeps kids in school-welcome news after districts have spent many years touting harsh zero-tolerance policies."

In addition to the above, a local school district's plan for discipline should be a part of a "long-term goal of prison reduction through opportunities, mentoring, intervention, support and other education services." SPLC has, itself, observed the over punishment of students of color and those with disabilities. These two groups are especially subject to this new federal scrutiny.

The Every Student Succeeds Act provides a most useful tool to dismantle this school-to prison pipeline. But a single piece of legislation will not eradicate inequality in all school districts. And there is some real concern that even this legislation fails to provide federal authorities with the kinds of tools that this law will require. There certainly is still much work yet ahead.

Christian Science Monitor's "EqualED"

A full page ad in the October 3, 2016 issue of the journal offers every reader an opportunity to become a member of this new effort by CSM to follow these trends in the weekly newspaper. "Tired of hearing about failing schools and the broken US education system? So are we. Welcome to EqualEd, a new section from The Christian Science Monitor."

"It's time for all our kids to have a chance at the future they deserve, regardless of race or ZIP *code."* Their veteran team will be conversing with students, parents, teachers, and policymakers about how they're creating a pipeline to opportunity inside and beyond the school. With a focus on "early learning, reinvented classrooms, and mentoring...Join us and be part of the solution."

The ad then gives the reader a way to sign up for their newsletter to get their latest videos, podcasts, and reporting. In addition, those who do take this seriously, will be invitations to special events and even volunteer efforts. The directions were very easy: Just Sign Up at csmegualed.com.

This is a good way for interested citizens to become much more knowledgeable about our public education system and how to help it reduce the all-too-evident Pipeline To Prison situation in our nation. I subscribe to the parent organization, Christian Science Monitor, even though I am NOT a member of its founding church. The quality of its weekly magazine and this new element are well worth your time.

'Ban the Box' Called for in Ohio

The 'box' is a small place in a job application. When checked, it means that the person applying for a job has been previously found guilty of a felony. When the box is eliminated from the application, the person applying now has the chance to demonstrate his/her own skills and knowledge. During invitational meetings with those doing the hiring, the candidate can now make known what he/she is able to do and there is the possibility of a new job.

A noted Ohio businessman in a guest column in the September 30, 2016 issue of the *Dayton Daily News* has called for Banning the Box here and beyond. Mark Holden contends that Ohio businesses should 'ban the box' because they are now cutting out of the labor market thousands of qualified workers. A few have already ceased to use the box and their choices among those previously found guilty of an offence have been given a real second chance in life.

Colleges are also being urged to 'ban the box' from their application forms.

When there, the chances for positive education are also removed. Students have the chance to also add to their credentials and to strengthen their own status in the job search process. Mr. Holden is general counsel and senior vice-president for Koch Industries.

My own requirements after I was released from prison included 100 hours of Community Service. After hours and hours of applications, calls, offers of Free help, etc.---no luck.

I was WITHOUT any call backs due to my former incarceration. I had kept my Probation Officer fully informed sending him copies of applications, notes on calls, etc. I was even told not to attend two different churches. He helped by enabling my Judge to see my work on this book and the Judge accepted it as meeting my CS requirement. Along with my wife, I am now an active member of Christ Church United Methodist in Kettering, OH with a wonderful outreach approach to my felony and my past as a part of their Christian Religion.

Psychologist Helps in San Quentin Prison

This was first heard on Sunday National Public Radio and then sent to me via email on Wednesday, October 5, 2016. The headline read: "Psychologist Helps San Quentin Prisoners Find Freedom Through Self-Reflection." Mr. Jacques Verduin knows most of the men in San Quentin by name. And now he's "trying to make sure that when they leave the California state prison just across the San Francisco Bay in Marin County, *they don't ever come back.*"

"Verduin-a tanned man with silver hair, in his mid-50s-has been running rehabitation programs inside San Quentin for two decades. All it takes is a visit to one of his classes, offered once a week for an hour, to see he's doing something different." The nonprofit program, called GRIP, or Guiding Rage into Power, runs for 52 weeks. "In the third week of class, the group gets a pretty simple but important homework assignment. Write down why you're here and what you want out of this whole thing. One by one they stand and read their answers."

"I'm here in GRIP to receive and gain some insight about myself and the crimes I've committed," says one man named Darrell. Another, named Noah, says he's here "because all the cool kids are doing it. That might mean there's something to it. If it's helped them, maybe it can help me."

Verduin explains to the group that what they're going to discover is a new kind of emotional muscle, just like the muscles they build up by weightlifting in the prison year. "Anger has an anatomy to it," he says. "It gets unbearable enough that-boom-I do something I never even thought about. But if you can learn to read it then you have some choices."

Now, you would think that such men, many of them convicted murderers, hard guys who have led hard lives, would not be into the idea of meditation and self-help. "But the waiting list to get into GRIP is 500 names long."

A man in for torture and robbery describes how the program has been a help for him. "You know, you go do your time and get out. You go in with no self-help, you get out with no self-help. Here, they always have it available for you to get, and once you get it, it's up to you to use it." And he also says the program is helping him learn about himself.

The GRIP program seems to be working and is expanding throughout California. Fifty one graduates have been released and none of them has returned to prison, even though the recidivism rate in the state is 45 percent.

Education comes in many forms and shapes both inside and outside of prison walls. But it is potentially vital to those who make a genuine effort to let it become a part of their life and living. True reform of our Prison (Jails too) System, MUST include improved access to quality learning opportunities.

The beauty of this is that there is room for a great deal of imagination and invention of the process. The opportunity is there and I want to be among those who have NO BOX for **any** of my readers to check

CHAPTER 8

Medical Mis-Practices w/ $$ Costs

Medical care is a fundamental right of all prisoners in the jails and prisons of this nation. Every man,woman, and child is fully protected in this right and they or their families have filed many successful lawsuits when their medical care was not carried out. This chapter will point out just a few of the malpractices engaged in by our jails and prisons: local,state and federal. The costs to taxpayers have been huge!

The Southern Poverty Law Center (SPLC) has just published a major report on the medical issues involved in all types of prisons throughout the United States. While this report deals with a private firm which contracts with all types of prisons to provide 'medical care' on a pay-per-head count basis with countless state and local prisons and jails, it clearly states its problems as a business factor.

Much of what follows at some length is taken from this report which shows how a profit goal can be twisted to result in flagrant malpractice cases over and over. "A dime less spent is a dime more profit" seems to be the prime result! The major fault in this entire medical field is found in this simple fact: *The U.S. Constitution says that ALL prisoners/inmates are fully entitled to have their medical needs provided in a timely fashion.* No ifs/ands/or buts about it. The government MUST be responsible for providing these constitutional rights to inmates no matter what type or level of jail or prison in which they are assigned.

This is one of the most significant rights that each prisoner has and which the institution is fully responsible to provide. What follows in this chapter will show in some detail just how often and at what cost to tax payers failure to provide adequate medical services, medicines, and treatments has occurred. Please read slowly and with care! You will be, I am sure, shocked by the disregard of this prisoner's individual needs.

SPLC October 27, 2016 Report

"Profits vs. Prisoners: How the largest U.S. prison health care provider puts lives in danger" by Will Tucker is the title of this lengthy report.

"Kelly Green was off the medication he needed for his schizophrenia and was talking about killing himself. Alarmed by the homeless man's erratic behavior on a cold Oregon night in February 2013, a convenience store clerk called the police." They came, arrested on a misdemeanor warrant and took him to the Lane County Jail. There Green, cursed and talked to inanimate objects." A booking deputy wrote in her notes:

"May be bipolar/schizophrenic. No meds...talks to himself...not making sense." But no one chose to act on his behalf.

"Although the prison health care giant Corizon Health Inc. had a contract to provide health screening and medical care at the jail, no one from the on-site Corizon staff made any effort to see Green or talk to him." He was placed in a cell by himself. He wasn't provided with any psychiatric treatment or given any medications.

> The next morning he snapped! Inside a 'courtroom in the jail' Green suddenly sprinted 10 feet toward a partition of concrete blocks with his head lowered. "As skull met concrete, it sounded like 'throwing a watermelon at the wall,' one observer later remarked." He suffered a catastrophic injury, later determined to be a 'burst fracture' of the C-4 vertebra in his neck. Corizon staff <u>chose not to send</u> him to a hospital. They wanted to delay that until after he was released and then others would "drop him off" at the hospital-a type of <u>'courtesy drop'</u>. Even this was not a medical action on their part-just a courtesy.

> "It was almost seven hours before Green was transported to the hospital. By then it was too late. He lost the use of his arms and legs,

> and was placed on a ventilator. He died from complications six months later.

"The life and death decisions made by Corizon staffers that day are the same kinds being made by the company's employees in state prisons and local jails across America- decisions that inevitably weigh a patient's medical needs against the cost to the company." This raises the question of whether Corizon and its competitors place profits over the health and safety of prisoners who have no chance to have any type of say as to who will be their medical provider. They also have no power to even seek such an opportunity in most cases.

The jury case on Green's injury, lack of treatment, and consequent death was finally settled when in July 2015. Corizon reached a financial settlement with Green's family. **"The terms are confidential."** But the results are so very obvious to anyone who cares.

Other Medical Problems with Settlements

Prison Legal News is a newspaper published monthly. Its veracity is very solid and much of the legal community subscribes to it. I have previously found it to be a significant source to use on almost any topic and medical treatment is certainly one of those categories. Please follow along as we simply look at major headlines from the **June 2016** issue. Study them for the medical needs exhibited but not provided and the costs that resulted. Some will be minor in dollars, but large in legal messages to those in charge of jails or prisons.

"$ 8,000 Settlement for Medical Maltreatment by BOP; Court Finds Experts Not Required." Derik Gilna wrote this short story about a federal prisoner, Michael Alan Crooker, who sued for a variety of problems. Bottom line: the court ruled, "However, where a plaintiff's claim is based primarily on a claim of negligent delay on the part of medical personnel, expert testimony is not necessarily required." He did get his glasses and treatment and a small settlement.

"Wrongful Death Suit Against Illinois Jail Survives Summary Judgment," also written by Derik Gilna. "According to the court, 'The Eighth and Fourteenth Amendments require prison officials to provide 'adequate food, clothing, shelter, and medical care' to prisoners, and take reasonable measures to ensure their safety." The court wrote that, "In this case, the defendant officers knew that the evening shift officers were so concerned about Gonzalez that several calls were made to the doctor...Thus they knew that his condition was objectively serious." The district court held the defendants' appeal was not frivolous. "The case remains pending." And when the details are presented in court, actions will be the likely result.

"Problems with California's New Medical Prison." written by Matt Clark. Even though it cost Californians $840 million to build this new location to house up to 3,000 patients. But infighting within the prison and a later decision to put $1.7 billion in medical treatment *on hold,* doomed the location to ever being effective. Later prisoner reductions also added to the problem. Taxpayer dollars spent but little accomplished was the result. Some good planning, but too much time and changes in leadership of the prison led to a major mis spending of "health dollars."

"New York Court of Claims Awards $1.75 Million to Prisoner's Estate." Written by Derek Gilna the story began when Scott Degina was sent to a local hospital for extensive tests. The hospital reported to the prison that they were to follow up on his condition regularly. In spite of the instructions, Degina developed urethral cancer which was metastasized to adjoining lymph nodes making surgery impractical. He died just 4 months before the court ruled in his favor. Courts do make good decisions, but time is not always appropriate.

"Illinois Prisoner Wins $125,000 Civil Rights Jury Verdict." Written by Derek Gilna, this story reported in both the discovery and trial portions that prison officials admitted that Mr. Lee had told them about his own fear of physical harm. Prison staff were also on notice. Lee showed that he had proven "actual knowledge of impending harm by showing that he complained to prison officials about a specific threat to his safety." Following payment of legal costs, Lee was awarded $99,466.10. Failure of officials to follow up on his medical concerns was costly.

July, 2016 Prison Legal News

"Breaking News: 18 Deaths in Six Months at Mississippi State Penitentiary." Written by Derek Gilna, the story explains that the deaths took place between November 10, 2015 and May 23, 2016. Only one was called a suicide. The ACLU has cited urgent problems in the state's prison system including deplorable conditions and sub-standard treatment for mentally ill prisoners.

"Supreme Court Allows Prisoner's 1983 Action after Dismissal of Federal Tort Claim. Derek Gilna wrote this complicated case. She concluded that the Court instead sided with Himmelreich (the prisoner), finding that the plain text of the FTCA's Exceptions section applied, because "Absent persuasive indications to the contrary, we presume Congress says what it means and means what it says." Thus the inmate's case just and he deserved the action.

Written by Rui Kaneya, Civil Beat, this is the lead headline and the much extended sub headline. "A Deadly Dust is Plaguing Hawaii Prisoners in Arizona; Valley fever is widespread in the Southwest, yet Hawaii prison officials haven't paid much attention to it, despite of at least two prisoners who had the disease." Eventually, Matt Murphy found out what was wrong. Wright had been suffering from a valley fever. "a disease caused by inhaling microscopic spores of a soil-dwelling fungus that thrives in the Southwest." Wright was not treated but was flown back to Hawaii, but it was too late. He died just a few days later. But the damage had been done and the prisoner was made suffer for it.

"Multiple Suicides at Florida Jail a Cause for Concern" by David Rutter. "Suicide is the leading cause of death among jail detainees according to an August, 2015 report by the U.S. Bureau of Judicial Statistics." ACJ officials refurbished the cells to prevent future suicide attempts. "Yet if guards fail to perform their duty to monitor the most bound and determined prisoners, such measures would fail to stop those who want to kill themselves." Too little, too late for too many would depend upon adequate guard supervision and training.

"Seventh Circuit Reverses Dismissal of Federal Prisoner's *Bivens* Suit Over Medical Care." Derek Gilna, who wrote this short story, noted that Ryan K. Mathison was incarcerated at a Federal Corrections Institution in Pekin, IL near Peoria. The Court of Appeals released some of the people charged, but maintained others as being more involved. "The case law required the prison to provide more than just basic medical care. Mathison's **$505** appellate filing fee was granted. The case remains pending.

"DC Prisoner Awarded $70,000 for ADA Violations at CCA-run Jail." William Pierce, a prisoner held by the District of Columbia's Department of Corrections (DCDOC) has won a *$70,000* jury verdict for repeated violations of the Americans with Disabilities Act (ADA). "Pierce who suffers from severe hearing loss, was denied hearing aids and sign-language interpreters while he was held at the Correctional Treatment Facility, a jail managed by Corrections Corporation of America (CCA)." Derek Gilna was the author.

September, 2016 Prison Legal News

"$81,200 for North Carolina Prisoner's Estate in Breach of Duty Suit." No author was assigned to this short story. The North Carolina Industrial Commission awarded the amount to the estate of a prisoner who died after a guard at the Greene Corr. Institution denied him medical care. Another case of negligence by prison staff for medical care that resulted in dollars for his estate.

"Mentally Ill Oregon Prisoner's Wrongful Death Suit Settles for $7.4 Million." Mark Wilson wrote this story for the issue. "Kelly Conrad Greene II suffered from paranoid schizophrenia. He was hospitalized in 2012 after expressing that he planned to kill himself by breaking his neck." Sometime later after Greene's death in June 2015 "Greene's family settled their claims for $7 million and the county agree to pay $500,000." A major settlement due to the failure of the state's medical staff to adequately provide for his medical needs.

Matt Clarke's article was headlined, "Jail Prisoner's Death Results in $1Million Judgment against Texas County." On October 25, 2015 a Federal Jury awarded $1million to the survivors and estate of a prisoner who died in a Texas jail, finding jail employees were deliberately indifferent to his medical needs." Terry Lynn Borum, 53, had been previously wounded by a shotgun blast during "a suicide attempt that left his face disfigured and his speech difficult to understand... He was mentally ill, depressed, and alcoholic." A federal jury found the county to have been deliberately indifferent to Broum's serious condition." More costs to the state and only because of its failure to provide care.

"Sexual Assault Victim Awarded $1.5 Million in Lawsuit against Illinois Prison Guard." was the headline for this article written by Christopher Zoukis. "A longtime Illinois Department of Corrections (ILDC) guard (Timothy Ware) was ordered to pay $1.5 million to a female prisoner he had raped, though he did not face criminal charges for the assault." The act took place against 25 year old Ashley Robinson in a supply closet. Not reported initially, he was later found guilty of seven felony counts. And her lack of proper care and medical services were a key part of this settlement.

"Allegheny County Reaches $2.09 Million Settlement for Prisoner's Death." Derek E. Black, 28 was denied medical care at Pennsylvania's Allegheny County Jail. Guards made many requests on his behalf but they were denied. The final judgment came when the County canceled appointments for 21guards to be scheduled for depositions. It seemed that the County 'threw-in' the towel when they had to NOT allow almost two dozen guards to testify. This is a case where the guards were doing the right thing all along and wanted the world to know that.

"Wrongfully-convicted Former Prisoner Receives $13.2 Million in FBI Hair Analysis Case." Writer Derek Gilina summarized this case: "A 53-year old man who was convicted based upon the now discredited 'science' of forensics hair analysis has been awarded $13.2 million by District of Columbia Superior Court Judge John M. Mott. This was the latest in a long line of cases where pseudo-scientific testimony by the FBI crime lab resulted in the wrongful conviction of an innocent defendant." Again, the case was a long one and it took much time for the final large settlement result to be made, but it was a case of mis-management of medical evidence.

"Prisoner's Healthy Kidney Erroneously Removed; Surgeon Receives Probation. Author for this story was David M. Reutter who said, "The California Medical Board place a doctor on three-years' probation for removing the wrong kidney during surgery on a federal prisoner." This violated all the rules for such surgery and when the error was 'caught' and the patient's bad kidney was then removed he was placed in severe danger of renal failure. But no$$$ were exchanged!

"Untreated Intoxication Death in Massachusetts Jail Results in $232,500 Settlement." There was no author for this short article. The City of Lowell, Massachusetts is now paying this amount for a sad case of medical neglect. An inebriated female was brought into the lockup but could not be understood. She was not helped, eventually was 'booked' with no ability to speak. Then was found dead. No medical care was given even though it could likely have saved her life. The court held that the denial of medical treatment was a key factor in her death and thus the settlement.

Conclusions

This "baker's dozen" examples from just three months issues of *Prison Legal News* has been used to provide readers with both major$$ claims and small cases. They have been selected to show the types of poor medical care that is being given throughout our nation. Large jails and very small ones have been shown. It is not the size that alone builds the problems.

In the Federal system, the issues are rather similar in that the care now provided varies dramatically from prison to prison, from where it is found, and from the attitude of the people who are in charge. My own care at Elkton near Youngstown was generally fine. I had no real complaints to record. Even though I was 77 and in good health for my age, I was given no special treatment for my 13.5 months of incarceration.

I am now 80 and had my blood tests very recently with AlC at 600, a full colonoscopy results from prison, and good vision. While still in prison I also had to use my scarce commissary funds to pay $2 per visit when I did have a need to be seen by medical staff. For me that was no problem, for others it meant they did NOT go to medical because they had no 'money'.

BUT I am very aware of some men with difficult situations. One man discovered that his medical records were no longer totally his own. His file and the file of another man had been intermixed with neither one being accurate. When Charles needed to be seen by a good eye doctor who could help him be able to see more completely, it seemed to be impossible. Yet his inability to see when looking outside his normal vision pattern could not be addressed. Thus his desire to learn to read was seriously inhibited. He was a volunteer for my "free" tutoring for his GED work.

Patient care was expensive, but we had very few doctors on duty, with many nurses with limited authority to deal with serious problems. The dental situation was better, but they seemed to want to remove teeth rather than seek to save them. I was able to have my goal to keep my teeth "in vs. out" honored. So I still have all of my original teeth except for wisdoms.

I had absolutely NO contact with anyone in the Psychology area AFTER my one required visit to help them be sure that I was not thinking about suicide. Some inmates did have regular "Visits" with one or more of these folks, but they were not happy about them. I have no personal negative elements here except that all psych personnel were on call to respond to any "Lockdown" needs for them to become "inspectors" regardless of their regular duties.

This removal of them from their normal medical duties not only slowed down the medical system, it tended to build distrust when they and other non-guards made gross errors on doing the new "shakedown" duties. Such mistakes as throwing out Bibles, Korans, etc. as well as removal of medicines from inmates were among the most significant errors. It was my observation that the prison medical situation was hampered by too few staff for an overcrowded institution and too many less than well trained for the non-medical tasks that too often were made necessary by the management of the prison. The increasing range of age of our prison population (more very young and more elderly like myself) made their work more difficult as well.

But the Constitution is very clear that the prisons and jails are all responsible for the medical needs and services and to delay or deny them is against the basic laws of our nation.

CHAPTER 9

Making Punishments Fit the Crime

When does punishment fit the crime? How do we know when there is a match between the crime and the punishment? When such a match does not occur, what are the opportunities to make some type of correction? How do we determine when there is a mis-match and then how do we resolve the discrepancy?

Julie Watson wrote this short article for the Associated Press which was published in the *Dayton Daily News* on May 3, 2012. The attention grabbing headline read, "Man forgotten in holding cell for four days." The sub-head gave more information: "Student was never charged, held with no food or water."

"San Diego—A college student picked up in a federal drug sweep in California was never arrested, never charged and should have been released. Instead, authorities say, he was forgotten in a holding cell for four days." Without any food or water and without any access to a toilet, Daniel Chong had to drink his own urine. The drug sweep did produce enough that Chong was handcuffed and placed back in the same cell, "a 5 by 10 foot windowless room."

Days later, paramedics took him to a hospital "where he was treated for cramps, dehydration, a perforated esophagus (from swallowing a glass shard) and kidney failure," his lawyer said. In 2013 Chong settled with the government for $4.1 million and many apologies.

Our prison system is a very busy and complicated process, but being left in a special holding cell for four days with no sustenance or water is beyond understanding. Nothing could possibly have been more of a miscalculation of punishment for whatever was his supposed crime. That the money he was awarded was not even close to 'paying' for what he had experienced.

Jailhouse Nation

The Economist for June 20, 2015 featured "Jailhouse nation: 2.3 million reasons to fix America's prison problem." for its cover story of that issue. No author is ever cited for this key article. The sub-head read: "America's bloated prison system has stopped growing. Now it must shrink." The cost to the American taxpayer has been estimated at $34,000 per inmate per year for a total bill around $80,000,000,000 (billion.)

"No country in the world imprisons as many people as America does or for so long." This results in the figures above. But another way to look at the situation is to observe the breakdown of the figures by race. "America, with less than 5 % of the world's population, accounts for around 25% of the world's prisoners. The system is particularly punishing towards black people and Hispanics who are imprisoned at six times and twice the rates for whites respectively."

The lockup of blacks and Hispanics are especially poor for these folks. Locked up with prison conditions which have no proper access to training, education or rehabilitation contribute to their lack of ability to cope with the outside world facing them upon release. Add to the above the many problems with medical treatment and care which these minorities are especially in need of in good quantity and quality and you have a major problem in the making.

"But even with a political appetite for reform and a public mood conductive to it, comprehensive cutting back will be hard. The expanded prison system has built itself into the fabric of society. Judges, district attorneys, state and county-level politicians, police forces, prison-guard unions, federal agencies and private firms that build and run prisons: all have contributed to the rise of mass incarcerations, and many benefit from it. In rural parts of America prisons are now the biggest employers in many towns."

All of these groups become major lobbying forces at both state and federal government levels. They represent real factors that act to slow down any significant decreases in prison population as jobs and sales will suffer if prison population is seriously reduced and private prisons are put out-of-business.

Such problems of these are made even worse when the facts that treatment of drug problems have gone almost totally unheeded. Men (and women too) when their time for return to the streets is reached have almost no skills acquired in prison to give them even a reasonable chance on the outside.

When a new crime bill signed by President Bill Clinton "met the street" so-to-speak, it was found to have banned prisoners from receiving Pell grants which had previously been available to them. This action along with other cuts in vocational training had seriously under-cut educational funding in prisons. People in charge have actually fought against such changes which has made the problems much more complicated.

Some money being spent formerly on prisons has now been moved to crime prevention. It now provides weekend gyms with carefully planned activities designed to change attitudes, skills, and habits. "If prison is to be less of a part of American life, the philosophy behind such schemes needs to spread…A system that has been designed to react to crime and to punish it, needs to prevent it instead. This will take a broad change in culture, not just tweaks to laws."

This means we need to have major efforts to build a coalition of all pertinent parties to plan for the changes that are ahead of such a major societal change. We need to be meeting with our schools, our chambers of commerce, our leaders, our ministers, our social workers, and all other groups we can muster to develop workable plans for addressing the treatment needs rather than just the incarceration needs.

Other Plans Out There

On December 12, 2016, a plan to locate a halfway house was reported by Cornelius Frolik in the *Dayton Daily News.* The story's headline read, "Dayton halfway house plan ignites controversy." Its sub-head told more of the story: "Agency official says crime is reduced where treatment centers exist." A solid idea but in spite of evidence to the contrary there will be some opposition. The subhead has the real message to be made primary.

An editorial in the *New York Times* April 10, 2016, called for "A Fair Chance After a Conviction." "Last week, for example, the Department of Housing and Urban Development warned private landlords that blanket bans on renting to people with criminal convictions—common throughout the country—violate the Fair Housing Act and can lead to lawsuits and charges of discrimination." Much more work for ambitious lawyers lies ahead on this because such bans blanket too much of our country.

"Another area of marginalization has been in higher education. There is no doubt that inmates who receive college degrees in prison—or even attend classes without graduating—are far less likely to end up back behind bars once they leave." The bottom line now falls on the Pell Grants which the congress has now made persons in prison ineligible to acquire. A change in those requirements now becomes essential because the denial of such grants is like adding years to the court's assigned time behind bars.

Also being locked out of society, labels like 'felon' are an unfair life-sentence according to another *New York Times* editorial of May 8, 2016. This problem is even more long-term in its impact since it refers to the refusing the right to vote in many states. Such simple use of more humane words could in the future make a big difference. Mr. Ellis, who died in 2014, made so very clear that "those extra few words acknowledged the humanity of people who having paid their debts, should not have to feel shut out forever."

In another editorial in the *New York Times,* (also on May 8, 2016) this one addressed the racially-based Virginia ban of life-time non-voting for anyone with a felony conviction. When Gov. Terry McAuliffe decided to pardon 200,000 former "felons" by pardoning them, the legislature had to decide whether or not to charge him instead. Virginia, along with Iowa, Florida, and Kentucky are the only 4 states that still prohibit all convicted felons from ever voting.

Mary Mogan Edwards wrote a story for the *Columbus Dispatch* which was published by the *Dayton Daily News* on June 3, 2016. The headline read, "Colleges urged to 'ban the box' on applications," but the sub-head also read, "According to the Education Department, schools that admit ex-offenders don't have crime rates larger than those that prohibit them." This would be just one less hurdle to overcome for many who have already served their sentence and paid for their previous crime.

Back to the *New York Times* for another editorial of August 14, 2016 entitled, "Echoes of Jim Crow for Georgia Voters." It seems that in another attempt to restrict voting in the state, the town council in Sparta, GA. voted to restrict the number of blacks in order to give a more favorable white vote in the local mayoral election. Police were required to go out and bring in 53 black voters to verify in person their right to vote. Some 27 did get their voting right back, but many others did not. It seems that Jim Crow did still work in Sparta, GA.

What Children Endure

In a *New York Times* column on July 10, 2016 under the heading, "Police Under Attack," and a headline that read: "What Children Endure in the Violent Collisions of Policing and Race." Yamicie Alcindor's article picked up many inches of precious newspaper space. The opening two paragraphs present a heart-rending story very appropriate for the reader to consider.

"In the past week alone, there was the 4-year old girl in Falcon Heights, Minn., who was captured on video consoling her mother after they watched a police officer shoot the mother's boyfriend through the window of a car. And there was the 15-year-old boy in Baton Rouge, La., who sobbed uncontrollably in front of television cameras after the similar shooting death of his father."

"Then there were the four brothers, ages 12 to 17, whose mother was shot by the sniper who opened fire on the police officers in Dallas on Thursday night while the family was protesting police violence against blacks. The mother who survived threw herself atop one boy as the others ran for their lives."

She goes on to describe the trauma of children who while the adults around them protest and demand justice reform. "Young witnesses of the carnage are reeling from their losses and harboring pent-up depression that often comes pouring out in panic attacks and breakdowns, relatives say." These 'fallouts' of police actions have lasting negative impact upon the communities involved and serious problems for these families.

"Fear of cops, and fear for them, fuel cruel summer," was the July 11, 2016 headline by three Tribune News Service writers. Rick Montgomery, Scott Canon, and Mara Rose Williams wrote their own observations of these events. "They know that these horrific episodes are not tied to one thing, but many: Racism, Cellphones, Political and cultural polarization, Guns, Economic inequality. Hate, Fear, Powder-keg news coverage." Given the original 'crime' that was not even likely to result in anything more than a fine, this is a major increase in the results that the community will have to face.

Punishment That Doesn't Fit the Crime

The headline just above served as the opening lead for the *New York Times* story on July 31, 2016. An opinion piece by Eric Berkowitz, it opened many eyes to the nature of the problems of this past summer. He writes about a young boy aged 11 who was hauled out of his fifth grade Texas classroom and charged with "indecent exposure."

This put him into a court system that provided him with a LABEL for LIFE as an official sex offender. Given the times, the label for life seemed very appropriate for having felt the need to go to the bathroom while his home's power was out and no bathroom was working. The phone calls, the taunts, the looks of hate, and the names he was now called ALL seemed so inappropriate for the boyhood action he had taken. They were! But they still are wrong! And the problem is a misplaced punishment that vastly over-fit the crime. Common sense seems to be been totally absent in such decisions.

When the national leaders passed the federal law, Adam Walsh Child Protection and Safety Act in 2006, it changed the world. Now even very young children were subject to the law and the law required them to be identified as Sex Offenders even for a simple act of going to the bathroom outside the house. This law still exists but more lawyers are now taking a new approach to such cases. And their numbers need to grow dramatically. Restoring common sense is a major need in our society today.

First of all, the results of the law are now much better known with criminals being permanently banned from housing in many cities for example. Secondly, the recidivism rate for such "behaviors" is much lower that for adult sex offenders. Because the sex laws now on the books have grown into a tangled mess of conflicting regulations and requirements many prosecutors like Vickie Seidl of the Kent County office in Michigan "now push for pleas that keep youths off registries. Other prosecutors are following suit."

The July 30, 2015 *New York Times* article by Doug Deason told about his own experience at a 'second chance.' When at age 17 he used the neighbors key to host a party at their place while they were out of town. It did not go well and he was in line for a lot of time in prison. Fortunately his lawyer was good and got a reduced plea with even that expunged from the record in time.

Now the leader of a major Texas company, he now makes sure that his company seeks out as new employees those who have a 'jail time' record but good behavior. He wants and has found that such 'second-chances' for others pays off for his business world. Now he meets with others such as the Koch brothers to talk about how to reduce crimes on the books and to give more people a "second chance." He wants to avoid the headline given to this article, "Ruining Lives with 'Justice'".

More and more employers are taking just such actions and are seeking former prisoners for jobs that are available. Banning the Box on application forms has been one very helpful step in that the ex-con will bring up his past and his success in an interview. This is a right step ahead for those former felons who now seek to be a productive part of society.

Research Studies Don't Hold Up

The *New York Times* article by Benedict Carey on August 28, 2015, was headlined, "Psychology's Fears Confirmed: Rechecked Studies Don't Hold Up." Now a 'recheck' of 100 leading studies has produced the whirlwind effect for the field of psychology. "The vetted studies were considered part of *the core knowledge by which scientists understand the dynamics of personality, relationships, learning and memory."*

Scientists rely on such studies to form the foundation for much of the pedagogical research now being done in this field. Many of these studies have become the basis for new laws and punishments BUT which are now being seriously questioned. In a few cases, the second look involved a larger number of respondents which thusly increased the 'sample size' and might have accounted for some of the changes noted.

"Police stingray cases challenged," was the lead headline for an article by Brad Heath in the *USA Today* paper of August 28, 2015. "Defense lawyers in Baltimore are examining nearly 2,000 cases in which the police secretly used powerful cellphone tracking devises and they plan to ask judges to throw out 'a large number' of criminal convictions as a result."

The results have of a study with court records has "showed that the authorities used stingrays to hunt everyone from killers to petty thieves, usually without obtaining search warrants and they routinely sought to hide that surveillance from the people they arrested." This has put many police departments on the watch for how they may have put people at much risk over time. Many cases may now be very suspect. Increasingly many lawyers are now clearly challenging prosecutors use of such 'information without warrant'.

Another case of justice denied is from the *Dayton Daily News* of March 15, 2015 where the *New York Times* article by Matt Apuzzo was found. Its headline read, "Feds condemn profit-minded court policies," with a sub-head of "Practices lock poor people in cycle of fines, debt, jail."

In a letter to chief justices and court administrators, Vanta Gupta, the Justice Department's top civil rights prosecutor who leads a program on court access, "Warned against operating courthouses as for-profit ventures. It chastised judges and court staff members for using arrest warrants as a way to collect fees...Such policies, the letter said, make it more likely that poor people will be arrested, jailed, and fined anew—all for being unable to pay in the first place."

Such actions have been shown to become "debtors prisons" and "cash cows" for a local jurisdiction. Public trust in the courts has been diminished as a result and changes are beginning to be made by many jurisdictions.

All of this has been preamble to a new Justice Department ruling expected soon. This has been designed to eliminate "debtor prisons" being reinstituted within the U. S. and the Justice Department is being very supportive as of 2016.

Michigan Sex Offender Law Dented Retroactively

The Sixth Circuit Court of Appeals in the federal system has just overturned parts of the Michigan's law on "after incarceration release" elements. Serving the states of Michigan, Ohio, Kentucky, and Tennessee, this decision is that parts of the 2006 and 2011 federal laws cannot be applied to persons convicted prior to those implementation dates. (More on this dramatic change in Chapter 13.)

But bottom line---many men will now be able to live more freely as a citizen and some even be able to vote in an election. Keep reading for much more on this topic very important topic regarding sex offender laws.

CHAPTER 10

Judges

Too often even where Judges are elected, they are often found somewhere near the bottom of the list of other officers which also demand voter attention. Several studies have shown the number of voters who actually vote on a given Judge contest is much below the number of people who have voted for much "higher" offices. NAACP of Greater Dayton (OH) is just one of the groups to be taking on how to improve the "value" of the vote for these offices as well.

First, they found that no judges in Ohio at least are allowed to show a party affiliation on the ballot. Thus, the most basic clue as to a political affiliation of a candidate is not readily available to a voter. Second, they found that the two main parties do not even create adds for a judicial candidate. It almost seems as though the parties prefer to keep these positions as non-political as possible. Why?

In our societal political view the judiciary and individual judges are thought to be non-political and the public likes it. However, when a judge must make a decision on an especially significant case, then there is often a loud cry for more information about Judge X. Sometimes, there is even the creation of plans to organize a "vote against" this judge at the next election.

The goal of the work of the local NAACP in Dayton is to prevent such negative actions on a judicial election by increasing the voter awareness of judges who are currently up for a vote. What this group is doing is seeking ways to help provide such information to voters well in advance of an election. Their goal is to have voters be more informed.

Judge Roy Moore, Georgia

One such case has been underway in Georgia since the appointment of Roy Moore as a State Circuit Judge in 1992. Alabama Chief Justice Roy Moore has continuously advocated his own personal position that any U.S. Supreme Court decisions do not hold in Alabama. He has further issued directives to all local Probate Judges that they have a personal and strong right to refuse to issue licenses for gay or lesbian weddings.

Several major legislative bodies have made regular attempts to bring such actions under the jurisdiction of the State Courts. The Southern Poverty Law Center (SPLC) and the American Civil Liberties Union (ACLU) have both been very active on this case for many years. Judge Roy Moore, also known as The Ten Commandments Judge followed the same religious beliefs to object to the 1963 rulings by the Supreme Court. More recently, he has been focused on the LBGT issues.

A major article by Kim Chandler of the Associated Press was printed by the *Dayton Daily News* on October 1, 2016. The large headline read: "Gay marriage stance costs Alabama chief justice his job." The sub-headline was: "State judiciary court rules that official defied the law."

The two lead paragraphs read: "MONTGOMERY, ALA Alabama Chief Justice Roy Moore was removed from the bench Friday for defying the U.S. Supreme Court on gay marriage, more than a decade after he got in trouble for refusing federal orders to move a Ten Commandments monument."

"By suspending Moore for the rest of his term, the nine-member Alabama Court of the Judiciary has effectively removed him office for the second time." The outspoken Christian conservative had been removed from office for disobeying a similar court order in 2013 for his stand in removing a 2 ½ ton monument of the 10 Commandments in the state's judicial building. But voters later re-elected him! He is now out of that job!

"The 50-page decision indicated that a majority of justices wanted to completely remove Moore—not just suspend him without pay—but they did not have the unanimous agreement." This punishment for Moore occurs at a time when all three branches of Alabama's government face major setbacks.

The Republican speaker of the state House of Representatives was removed from office this past summer for criminal violations of ethics. A legislative committee is considering whether or not that Gov. Robert Bentley should be removed via an impeachment over a scandal involving a key top aide.

"Moore was elected to be a judge, not a preacher. It's something that he never seemed to understand. The people of Alabama who cherish the rule of law are not going to miss the Ayatollah of Alabama," said Richard Cohen, President of Southern Poverty Law Center. This penalty effectively removes him from this job for good since he is now 69 and current law any new term beginning when a candidate is 70.

This case resulted in the removal of Chief Justice Roy Moore from his *elected* seat on the State Supreme Court by a Judicial Review Board. Just recently, he ran for nomination, was a winner, and must now be considered for the U.S. Senate as his party's representative in a special general election. Judges are not immune from voter decisions.

Inmate Gets More Time for Threatening Judges

The Columbus Dispatch's writer, John Futty, tells the story about an inmate who sent anthrax letters to two judges. "An Ohio prison inmate had three years *added* to his sentence on Monday for sending hoax anthrax to two Franklin County Judges."

"Sean A. Helso, 33, was serving a 30-year prison term for a series of armed robberies committed around the state when he sent the judges threatening letters last year containing a powder that he claimed was anthrax." Then Helso pleaded guilty to possession or use of a fake material which could be "a weapon of mass destruction, retaliation, intimidation, and inducing panic."

The judge then sentenced him "to three years in each case, to run concurrently, as recommended by prosecuting and defense attorneys in a plea agreement." In addition he was also sentenced to an additional 60 days in County Jail for spitting on a nurse who was treating him at that time. Helso later apologized for his actions.

We do take legal steps to protect our judges and in this case, use the courts to add to his sentence several more years to be served. Our society supports this aspect of our Judicial System and some might even want more retribution to be enacted.

Another SPLC Action

On September 28, 2016 "The anti-LGBT hate group *Family Research Council (FRC)* is planning to announce legislation today pushing for the repeal of the amendment to the U.S. tax code that prohibits certain nonprofits and churches from weighing in on elections. The so called "Johnson Amendment," which evangelicals and the conservative right have targeted for years, prohibits churches and other nonprofit organizations with 501©(3) designations under federal tax code from endorsing and opposing political candidates. FRC is proposing the Free Speech Fairness Act to overturn the restrictions." Ryan Lenz summarized this effort to coincide with the attacks on Chief Judge Roy Moore on the same date in Georgia.

In an article discussing Trump's interest in getting rid of the Johnson Amendment, *The Atlantic* noted that while Congress first approved tax deductions for donations to charitable organizations in 1917, "the boundaries around those organizations' political activities weren't exactly clear." The Johnson Amendment clarified that ban extended to political activity: "Non-profits, including religious groups, couldn't support candidates for political office without losing their tax-exempt status," *The Atlantic* wrote.

The Atlantic article summarized the results on the American political system if the Johnson Amendment were to be overturned. "(P)astors would be able to endorse candidates from the pulpit, which they are currently not allowed to do by law. But it is also true that a lot more money could possibly flow into politics via donations to churches and other religious organizations. That could mean religious groups would become much more powerful political forces in American politics—and it would almost certainly tee up future court battles."

The Johnson Amendment is a very hot political issue in Washington, DC right now. The conservative far right is fighting very hard to get Congress to overturn it and to allow the churches to collect and pay for political ads for and against candidates and issues. The more liberal left is just as strongly opposed to this action and fighting equally hard to protect the Amendment.

Justice reform is very much a part of this issue. The chances for new laws on the nature of prisons, who should have educational opportunities, and how to make our sentencing more appropriate for the crime committed are all connected to this Johnson Amendment issue.

Judge Aaron Persky Recall Effort

Judge Persky is an American judge sitting on the Superior Court of California, County of Santa Clara. Prior to joining the bench, he practiced civil litigation for five years and was a prosecutor in Santa Clara County for six years. He is now facing a major effort to remove him from the bench for a decision he made in a sex attack case in 2016.

He was a Phi Beta Kappa from Stanford University in 1984. After a Master's degree there he went on to law school at UC Berkeley School of Law in 1990. His law career included much time spent working on hate crimes and for the poor. In 1997 Persky joined the Santa Clara District Attorney's Office. He also served on the executive committee of the Support Network for Battered Women and the Santa Clara County for a Hate-Free Committee.

In his work for the county, he was re-elected in June 2016 to another six-year term on the bench in Santa Clara County. But in August 2016 he requested to be transferred from criminal to civil court as a result of the Brock Turner case.

The Turner case was very unusual in several aspects. Prosecutors sought a six-year term in state prison and the defense called for a 4-month term in county jail. The *pre-sentencing report* went for a 6-month term in jail citing Turner's youth, clean record, and what would be best for the young man. As he almost always did, Judge Persky followed the pre-trial report!

This report by a court officer is very thorough and covers the person charged, his school records including high school in Ohio, his adolescent behavior there and since here in California, grades, etc. These reports are typically very thorough and look at all aspects of the defendant and his case.

The uproar that has followed the trial and the sentencing has found many players taking positions for and against Judge Persky. He has now been forced to form a committee to fight the recall effort, called "Retain Judge Persky---No Recall". Whether or not this action to recall the judge is carried out, it does show that there can be limits and judges must consider public opinion.

Federal Judge: Sexual Orientation Law

A December 23, 2015 Associated Press article had this headline: "Federal judge: U.S. discrimination law applies to sexual orientation." U.S. District Judge Dean Pregerson found that a 1972 law prohibiting sexual discrimination at federally funded colleges and universities covers the women's claims that they were discriminated against because they were dating."

His reasoning was that if they were men dating women, no problem. But they were women dating other women at Pepperdine University and that was what had brought about the charges and actions. "But Pregerson cited an Equal Employment Opportunity Commission decision on another federal statute that says allegations of sexual orientation discrimination 'necessarily state a claim of discrimination on the basis of sex.'"

An attorney for the women said, "Pregerson's ruling reflects how the courts and society are taking a deeper look at issues related to gender and sexual orientation, noting the recent shift on same-sex marriage." The judge added, "If Plaintiffs had been males dating females, instead of females dating females, they would not have been subjected to the alleged different treatment."

When even the Federal Judges have to make crucial decisions, what is happening in the world around them becomes very important. This Judge clearly makes a distinction as to what is covered and not covered in human sexual relations. This type of awareness is vital for all judges be they federal or local IF judicial reform is to move forward.

Judge Elections Key, But Ohio Voters Snub Them

On August 14, 2016, Thomas Suddes wrote an opinion article for the *Dayton Daily News* in which he examined the headline just above. "As to Ohio judges, voters are presidents. Ohioans get to pick their judges. That's why utilities, insurance companies, defense lawyers in death penalty cases and General Assembly members who love safe districts pay close attention to Ohio judgeships. But not enough rank and file Ohioans do, despite what's at stake for them."

The voter stake centers in the state Supreme Court and the District Appeals courts. There is only one Supreme Court with 7 members and 12 District Appeals courts in the state.

Back in 2012 when President Obama was re-elected President, 70.5 percent voted in that race.

But the turnout for Ohio's three Supreme Court vacancies drew only 50 to 52 percent attention.

The low turnout in 2014 found 40.6 percent of the voters electing Kasich as governor in an unexciting race for sure. But the Ohio Supreme Court races attracted only about 33 percent of voters.

"Agreed, Ohio's judicial ballot makes it tough to figure out when a court candidate is close to a voter's philosophy—the polite word for biases. That's because the names of judgeship candidates don't also list their party affiliations on the ballot." The Dayton Area Unit of the NAACP is very concerned about this "fallout" of voters and is working to bring about more change in the future.

The NAACP is looking for many ideas to help it plan for the kind of actions that will give more voters more information about judicial candidates. This is a major effort of this local chapter of the organization, but it has potential benefit for all of Ohio and perhaps for our nation as a whole.

CHAPTER 11

Religion in Prison

When men or women are sent to prison or the jail, they have every right to expect that they will have a full and respectful way for them to continue to practice their own religion. That will include time for services, meditation, and practices affiliated with the religion. This is the normal anticipation given our Constitutions treatment of religion. Perhaps not every reader is aware of this, but the U.S. Constitution is very explicit when it says that all inmates in any prison or jail is fully entitled to be able to engage in the full exercise of his religious rights including ceremonies and activities of all types. This was quoted directly previously but repeated here as a reminder. But do these freedoms occur?

Such was not the case at a Bureau of Prison (BOP) facility. A man died while at the prison and his friends wanted a funeral service for him. The Head Chaplain was to be in charge of the service. What he planned and led was a "come-to-Jesus" service. The problem he faced (unknowingly?) was that the man was Islamic as were many of his friends. The real problem was that he was so involved and tied to his VERY fundamentalist views of religion that even the Catholics were suspected of not being Christian. No opportunity to share *the real religion* could be bypassed.

Religious Freedom or Freedom of Worship?

On July 31, 2015, Bishop Greorge V. Murry, S.J. wrote the article for *The Catholic Exponent,* Youngstown, OH area Catholics. He started his short writing by quoting the First Amendment. *"Congress shall make no law respecting an establishment of religion, or prohibiting the free exercise thereof."*

He then proceeded to inform his readers that the well-known phrase, "separation of Church and state" did not appear until Thomas Jefferson used it in an 1802 letter to the Danbury Baptist Association. It was his goal to say that the State could not interfere with religions. Our nation's goal was to remain neutral about them, but also to support them when and where possible.

Freedom of religion is very different from freedom of worship. Our people can live fully by their own religious beliefs and never interfere with the next persons right to do the same. But freedom of worship implies that a person may live the tenets of his or her religion, but ONLY in private "such as in a particular church, school, synagogue, or mosque."

The Bishop was showing his "constitutional support" for the Hobby Lobby case, but also demonstrating how that very case was so closely tied to how the government might or might not be trying to force the employees to accept an aid from an employer who did not believe in birth contraception.

But prior to the above, on November 14, 2014 Mary Ellen Pellegrini wrote an article also for *The Catholic Exponent* but this time pointing out how "Lutheran-Catholic Covenant Celebration offers reflections on theology of the cross." It was most interesting how these two different churches have been able to find time and ways to look at each others' beliefs and practices in such a reverent manner.

It also raised real questions for the men at the local BOP institution where in our small group were men from many different religions in general and several from former Lutheran and Catholic backgrounds in particular. The Lutheran Bishop, The Rev. Dr. Walter F. Taylor said that he felt that, "Both his and Father Bednar's presentations offered an understanding of theology of the cross in terms of how the two faiths traditions live together and may live together more closely in the future, as we all stand together at the foot of the same cross."

As a lifelong Lutheran, a council member, and a lay-leader I could not even imagine becoming active in the BOP head chaplain's view of Christianity. Therefore I became an integral part of the Catholic program at the institution. I sang in the choir as one of the five Protestants and four Catholics—very ecumenical. I was given communion along with all others who simply professed faith in the resurrection. Very ecumenical and very appropriate described the situation for me.

Race, History and Baptist Reconciliation

"With the protests in Ferguson, MO, the Black Lives Matter movement and the massacre of black church goers in Charleston, SC, on their minds, the presidents of the nation's two major Baptist groups—one predominately black—decided it was time for a bold gesture. The Southern Baptist Convention, founded by slaveholders and their supporters before the Civil War, is now the nation's second largest Christian denomination after the Roman Catholic Church." This is how the *New York Times* opened Laurie Goodstein's Conversation article in the January 24, 2016 paper.

"Fellowshipping is what he is talking about. We've agreed to that. He's absolutely correct: Suspicion, fear, distrust, all that stuff is there. How do you get beyond that if you don't get to know people.?" If the leaders of two parts of the same basic church must struggle to be able to get to know about each other how will prisons and jails ever be able to provide an opportunity for their members to practice their faiths whatever they may be?

Learning to live in this way is exactly what most prisoners will be expected to do on their own when their time to be released occurs. If it is not the goal of the BOP and of all jails and prisons, it should be.

Why Religion Still Matters

Mary Beth McCauley's cover story for the *Christian Science Monitor* of October 12, 2015 was filled with much information about our nation and its religious beliefs and customs. "Church attendance is down, but those who go are more devout. Here's what draws them." was her opening headline. She continued, "But, experts note, America is far from becoming a churchless nation. On any given Sabbath, for instance, some 4 out of 10 Americans will make their way to churches and synagogues, mosques and temples—a number that hasn't fluctuated dramatically in the past half century."

Samantha Evans, a Presbyterian pastor in Philadelphia observed, "At the end of the day, I think a lot of people are seeking understanding." Ms. Evans prays informally with members of the faith community who worship in the Presbyterian reformed tradition. Mitchell Marcus, a professor at the University of Pennsylvania who attends a conservative synagogue feels that, "Being human is hard and is challenging. Religion holds up for us an ideal behavior and ideal practices to strive for."

From such diverse backgrounds we find such solid views about how life should be lived outside within society. Do inmates have the opportunities to practice such behaviors while still in prison? If not, then the prison and jail "bosses" must turn thing around inside.

"More than 81 percent of Americans say they identify with a specific religion or denomination." was a mid-stream box headline. Emily Sullivan, a conservative Catholic observed this, "Culture is so noisy. Everything is 140 characters. But people need silence and time alone with their thoughts—to listen to that voice within." So do our nation's inmates if we hope to welcome them into our midst when they have served their punishment.

Tod Roulette, an African American art dealer who attends St. Phillips Episcopal Church in New York commented, "Not a lot of black gay men are drawn to that (Episcopalian) side of spirituality. They're missing a lot of depth." And another box heading read, "Americans are no less likely to attend church services today than they were in the 1940s and '50s."

But…life in prisons or jails

But in our prisons and jails, the same diversity is very much in place. Many are still very hungry for the type of discussions, spirituality, church service, collective effort, and worship that existed outside. Churches are very much a part of the service that can be provided to the prisoners, but you sometimes have to select something that is closest to you. Some attend an occasional event as they attend a Christian service vs. a Buddhist gathering just to support a friend who is being honored.

Being among the eldest in my housing unit at Elkton, OH BOP I was able to make friends with ease. I noticed a number of the Mexican males and began to follow the drawing that one man did so much of. I even bought a Spanish-English dictionary and tried to find words to describe his work and how much I admired it. One of his English speaking friends began to call me, "abuello," grandfather. I looked up the word for grandson, "nieto," and made this into our dialogue in the unit and out on the walks to and from places. Others overhearing us, picked it up and I became an unofficial grandfather to dozens. And some of them also began to attend the Catholic services which always were bilingual in nature. My two years of Spanish in the early 1950's were remembered and served me well among the inmates.

Each individual retains his/her basic fundamental religious rights **even when in prison.** During a 'lockdown' in prison, the BOP has explicit guidelines on just what can and cannot be taken from a cell or pad. For example, no guard or correction officer (can include teachers, psychologists, medical types, etc. etc.) is allowed to remove religious books or materials. This does not always happen! Some even took Bibles because they did not look like the Bible the "guard" new about (New Revised Standard Version with no 'thee's or thou's' for example).

While such problems created massive disruption and upset and were usually solved within a few days, they made no sense. When problems included services not being held or religious restriction being violated, the difficulties were compounded over time. For example, when a "shakedown" was taking place anywhere on campus, ALL classes were cancelled!

When basic constitutional human rights are disrespected while incarcerated, the system must be informed and held to be accountable. Fortunately, these cases are fewer and thus news of their resolution are also rare. But I am now aware of this problem and urge others to be more alert to such problems at both the federal and state levels.

We must all stand very tall for these fundamental rights of human beings who happen to be incarcerated. We must be sure that they are enabled to remain strong or to become strong in their faith so that they have a church home which will welcome them back and help them in their readjustment. I was very lucky to find such a church after being told to leave two others. I am once again helping with distribution of communion bread and wine several times a quarter.

CHAPTER 12

Eliminating Private Prisons

The reduction of Private Prisons as a part of the "landscape" for housing incarcerated men and/or women is now rising since the Federal government has just issued its order to close the systems of private prisons that it now has in operation. Carl Takei, ACLU National Prison Project, on August 12, 2016, wrote a major article for all members. This article also was originally posted at *The Marshall Project.* Key points will be made with plenty of quotes throughout since the topic is so crucial for this book.

"On Thursday, the U.S. Department of Justice inspector general released a scathing report on the Federal Bureau of Prisons' monitoring of 'contract prisons,' a shadow network of private, for-profit prisons that hold about 11 percent of the nation's 193,000 federal prisoners.

...Sentence by sentence, the report shows how the bureau fails to impose basic standards of health, safety, and human decency on the private companies it pays to run these prisons."

In one very telling example the inspector general relates about a prisoner who told the medical staff that his breathing was not good but that he was refused immediate care, told to fill out a written request for a medical appointment. Thus untreated, he died! The full report concludes, "Afterward, the Bureau of Prisons (BOP) conducted a mortality review that criticized this denial of care but did not propose any specific corrective action. As a result, ...'contractor deficiencies went uncorrected and corrective actions were delayed...putting other inmates at risk.'"

The 'at risk' –is a mild way of saying something like, "in danger of dying from causes that are easily treated." The prison population in such 'for-profit' institutions HAVE died from such ailments as untreated HIV, untreated cancer, suicide, and heart attacks/seizures where in-house leaders delayed hospital transfers. Other major inadequacies include the following:

- Using solitary confinement cells too much
- Understaffing
- Going without a full time physician for almost a year

"The inspector general also reports that the private prisons experience **nine** times as many lockdowns as bureau-run prisons and significantly higher levels of violence than bureau-run prisons."

Thus the evidence begins to just increase that turning over prison control and management to private (for profit) groups creates many serious problems for taxpayers and for the prisoners incarcerated within them. The public tends to lose control and the ability to make needed changes within such private places.

To prevent such abuses as these the inspector general created a set of recommendations to the bureau. It did not object to the suggestions as many were both sensible and necessary. However, they do not confront the basic question of should the bureau continue to use these "for-profit" institutions. In too many cases it was seen to be "more profitable" to pay the fine than to fix the problem.

For-Profit Prisons: Eight Statistics

Kevin Mathews developed a list of eight statistics which were first published on December 27, 2013. A noted author and contributor to Care2, his observations are well-worth your time to read them now almost 3 years later. He says in the introduction, "It's time society takes a look at the institutions and asks, 'Are prisons really being used as rehabilitation/deterrence for crime, or have private interests started attaching price tags to lawbreakers' heads and exploited their incarceration for profit?'" Care 2 is a major study group that investigates a number of topics that influence the public good. Private prisons is one such category of their work. *(www.care2.com/causes/for-profit-prisons-8-statistics-that-show-the-problems.html)*

I have decided to use his entire list and am quoting all but his contact information within each paragraph. I am also contacting 'Care2' and am now on its email list as well. I may well need to go back to a previous chapter in order to make use of materials found in this search. These 8 statistics were first 'published' by Care2.

"500% Increase

The biggest private prison owner in America, The Corrections Corporation of America, has seen its profits increase by more than 500% in the past 20 years. Moreover, the business' growth shows no sign of stopping, having already approached 48 states to take over government-run prisons."

"10-60 Pounds Lighter

One way for-profit prisons to minimize costs is by skimping on provisions, including food. A psychiatrist who investigated a privately run prison in Mississippi found that the inmates were severely underfed and looked "almost emaciated." During their incarceration, prisoners dropped anywhere from 10 to 60 pounds."

"100%

100% of all military helmets, ID tags, bullet-proof vests and canteens are created in federal prisons systems through prison labor. Though prisoners are 'generously' compensated cents per hour, it's clear having this inexpensive, exploited labor force is critical to the military industrial complex. I bet that the irony that mostly non-violent offenders are making war gear for others to perpetuate violence abroad without consequence is not lost on many inmates."

"90% Occupancy.

States sign agreements with private prisons to guarantee that they will fill a certain number of beds in jail at any given point. The most common rate is 90% though some prisons are able to snag a 100% promise from their local governments. Because of these contracts, the state is obligated to keep prisons almost full at all times or pay for the beds anyway, so the incentive is to incarcerate more people and for longer in order to fill the quota."

"More Laws and Longer Sentences.

One in every four people that is incarcerated worldwide is held captive in a United States jail. How is it that a country with only 5% of the world's population has 25% of all the inmates. Simple: prisoners are source of revenue for private companies, so the demand for incarcerating them is especially high."

"11 Times.

Violent crimes are down overall, so how does the United States keep prisons stocked instead? Amplifying the war on drugs: there are now **11 times** as many people in jail for drug convictions than there were in 1980 constituting 50% of the prison population. Longer mandatory minimum sentences also keeps the inmates in longer. Most people incarcerated for drug charges are non-violent, have no prior record, and are addicts rather than major drug-trafficers."

"50%.

Nearly half of all detained immigrants are held in privately owned facilities. The fact that ICE (Immigration and Customs Enforcement) has stepped up its game to detain more undocumented immigrants—about 400,000 each year has actually increased the need for private systems as most detainees will linger in the system waiting for court dates for months if not years. Civil rights groups have deemed the quality of care provide in immigrant detention centers unacceptable, particularly because of the large numbers of preventable fatalities and sexual assaults."

"$45 Million

The three largest for-profit prison corporations have spent more than $45 million on campaign donations and lobbyists to keep politicians on the side of privatized incarceration. In light of all of their ethical violations, it's obvious that they have to offer some incentive for keeping their business legal."

VICTORY—well sort of....

I recently received this detail email directly to me from the ACLU informing me and now you about this news from the Federal government. It is a significant advance on this issue of reducing our dependency on private prisons. Unfortunately, within about six months a new administration would be in office and would be looking to increase the number of such institutions in the US.

"August 20, 2016 9:37 a.m.
Hi James—
We just received extraordinary news.

VICTORY
Justice Department tells Bureau of Prisons: Begin phasing our private prisons now!

ACLU supporters like you have long demanded an end to inhumane, profit-driven prisons. This week was momentous—the Department of Justice ordered the Bureau of Prisons to phase out its use of private prisons.

The order includes shrinking what had been a planned contract renewal for five private prisons in Texas from 10,800 down to 3.600 prisoners. By May of next year, the Bureau of Prisons is expected to have 14,000 prisoners in private prisons, **a decline of about 50% from the peak a few years ago.** And as other contract renewals with for-profit prisons come up nationwide, the BOP will be instructed to reduce the numbers and, where possible, not renew the contract at all.

This is a sea change win—and **it wouldn't have happened without supporters like you!** Together with our petition partners Detention Watch Grassroots Leadership, and The Nation, we have taken a big step toward repairing America's broken criminal system.

Thank you for fighting for prison reform.
Anthony (Romero) for the ACLU Action Team"

This vital document which so carefully sets forth the essence of the Department's bold action, would not have been possible previously. This is a major step forward considering the previous work of Care2 and thousands of others from all parts of the nation and many from overseas as well. It does highlight the emphasis of the BOP and puts forth major action suggestions for the state DOCs all across our nation.

My hope is that this action escalates into a major type of national surge which will put significant emphasis upon the states to replicated. What happens due to the change of leadership in Washington, DC is open and must be watched very closely as the Current Attorney General Jeff Sessions has spoked clearly about wanting more people to be incarcerated.

CHAPTER 13

Sex Offender Punishments

Today's laws for those convicted of sex offenses especially against children have become a major problem for our society. For those who have served their punishments but now they find that they are now subjected to what can be an extended sentence for many years more. This must be changed.

A book review article by Mark Oppenheimer in the Friday *New York Times* was headlined, "Child Abuse Cases Endure as Lessons In Hysteria." The book, **We Believe the Children: A Moral Panic in the 1980s**, was written by Richard Beck. The reviewer begins by describing the McMartin case hyper reactions which ended up without a single conviction. Not even *60 Minutes* or *20-20* stories were able to bring about convictions. But the awareness and the hyper parents created "a social and political climate (which) fueled an epidemic of false accusations."

Oppenheimer writes, "Mr. Beck believes that an unholy alliance between anti-pornography feminists...and the Christian right fostered the overly fearful climate in which schoolchildren were lectured about 'good touch' verses 'bad touch' and adults could be easily accused of the latter."

"Mr. Beck concludes with a bit of Freudian psychology of his own, 'Recovered memory and the day care and ritual abuse hysteria drove the social repression of two ideas. First, the nuclear family was dying. Second, people mostly did not want to save it.'" It was easier to attack society "than to rescind no-fault divorce laws or to convince women to quit their jobs."

Thus the hysteria continued to grow and the punishments of those who offended became more and more complicated with many new examples of longer probation periods and more and more restrictive conditions added to the laws.

A sex offender could fully serve his time in prison and then be increasingly punished by new restrictions on where he could live, with whom he could live, and where he could go to be with his own children.

John Rosemond, a parenting columnist, produced a column on December 28, 2015, in the *Dayton Daily News* which was given this headline, "Think before photographing kids' bath." He continued, "Your friend's reaction to the photo as a tad over the top. Nonetheless, it is understandable given that general awareness of and sensitivity to the issue of sexual exploitation of children has risen significantly in the last 30 years or so."

An American veteran was given 'star' treatment by Anna Mulrine in her July 25, 2015 article for the *Christian Science Monitor.* The focus of her story was cybercrime and its headline read: "Vets fight a new enemy: child porn." The sub-head continued the story's main theme: "The HERO Corps is arming wounded veterans to help curb a rising online scourge." Nathan Cruz, a member of the HERO Corps responded to a question, "People ask me, 'How do you do it?' My answer is that pedophiles are worse than the Taliban." Hate is spread and its message continues within society and our justice system.

Why does all this matter? "After being all but eradicated in the US in the 1980s, child pornography has exploded in the Digital Age. In fighting it, some veterans—already trained to be tenacious and to cope with disturbing images—say they have found a new way to serve their country." The hope is that these men and women will be able to use their skills and tenancy learned in combat to provide manpower to the government with help in locating the porn whether it be in cellphones, dvds, thumb drives, laptops, etc. Prosecutors have been able to make good use of their skills and drive.

6th Circuit Issues Scathing Ruling

On August 26, 2016 the Appeals Court serving the 6th Circuit (Michigan, Ohio, Kentucky, and Tennessee) issued a scathing ruling against Michigan for its Sex Offender Penalties in an article by Mark Joseph Stern. One example of the extent to which the law had been extended involved school zones. A map that accompanied this story showed the "school zones" for Grand Rapids, MI.

Like so many states, Michigan seemed to have become almost addicted to punishing sex offenders—over and over and over again—long after they had been fully rehabilitated. These measures had been designed to shame, ostracize, and stigmatize the former felons. "On Thursday, the application of these laws to a large group of former offenders was invalidated by the U.S. Court of Appeals for the 6th Circuit in a **vitally important ruling** that suggests that the judiciary has finally begun to view draconian sex offender laws as the unconstitutional monstrosities they obviously are."

"Over the last decade, Michigan has amended its sex offender registry law to ensure that sex offenders are continually penalized for years after they complete their sentences. They are required to inform law enforcement *in person* when they wish to move, change jobs, enroll or unenroll as a student, change their name, register a new email address, or 'internet identifier,' travel for more than a week, or buy or sell a car." They are also barred from living, working or 'loitering' in a *school safety zone."*

"Their names, addresses, photographs, and biometric data are provided to the public in an easily searchable database. Some purportedly "serious" offenders must update law enforcement (again in person) with the most minute updates of their life every three months." Now that you have an idea of what many sex laws are all about, it is time to move on the what the Court actually said.

A group of persons who had prior to 2006 or 2011 been found to be sex offenders but now were being forced to meet all of these new regulations filed suit charging that they were afoul of the Constitution's Ex Post Facto Clause as well as its Due Process Clause. "In a unanimous ruling, a panel of judges for the 6th Circuit emphatically agreed. The Supreme Court has held that a law contravenes the Ex Post Facto clause when it is a 'criminal punishment,' not a 'civil regulation.'

A 2003 ruling also found that such retroactive rules and registration are civil and thus constitutional. "But, the 6th Circuit explained, Michigan's laws go far beyond that, constituting a 'byzantine code governing in minute detail the lives of the state's sex offenders.'" It went on to contend that the Michigan rules also have "much in common with banishment," and essentially exiting those who have previously broken the sex offender laws from urban centers. This constitutes an ongoing series of punishments that *punish* sex offenders for many years and perhaps for life. This is very Unconstitutional and must be corrected.

In addition to banning these laws as "onerous and retributive"—two hallmarks of a criminal penalty--"the court invalidated their application to any offender convicted before their enactment." The Court went further when it cited the scant evidence of such laws having any effect on reducing recidivism and thus keeping Michigan communities safer.

"Because the plaintiffs in this case won easily under an Ex Post Facto challenge, however the court left these broader constitutional questions for another day. Still the ruling should give other offenders a great deal of hope that the judiciary is finally pushing back against these unfair, unjust, and ineffective laws."

More on Michigan's Laws

From this same case came more about the Sex Offender Regulation Act (SORA) and its impact upon these persons. Jack Bouboushian wrote his article on August 26, 2016 for the *Courthouse News Service*. In addition to all of the information above, he used these quotes. "SORA brands registrants as moral lepers solely on the basis of a prior conviction. It consigns them to years, if not a lifetime, of existence on the margins, not only of society, but often, as the record in this case makes painfully evident, from their own families, with whom, due to school zone restrictions, they may not even live."

Judge Alice Batchelder said in writing for the three judge panel, "The retroactive application of SORA's 2006 and 2011 amendments to plaintiffs is unconstitutional, and it must therefore cease." These findings "will affect the lives of thousands of sex offenders residing in Michigan, as well as the circuit area including Kentucky, Ohio and Tennessee." Michigan has the fourth- largest population of sex offenders list with 42,700 registrants."

Blatant Disregard for Constitution

This decision by the court is the first to be made with the possibility of more circuit courts following suit. It has already brought news of the Attorney General considering an appeal for his state of Michigan but this is being viewed more as a delay tactic than an actual plan. The fact that being on an internet list makes an individual so very easy to locate and then to bother as former neighbors—now enemies—can keep track of where one lives, works, uses email, etc.

Keeping track of these people is now a game for many citizens who follow an offender's every move. Those who have responded to one of these postings have been given much trouble already and feel that they are continuing to be punished for many years beyond the "time they have already served."

In a September 7, 2016 posting by David Post, a writer for *The Washington Post,* leads off with this. "The decision (Michigan case) is an especially important one, possibly signaling…that the judiciary has finally begun to view draconian sex offender laws as the unconstitutional monstrosities they obviously are." He points out that "Judge Alice Batchelder—who is, incidentally, a George W. Bush appointee widely regarded as one of the leading 'conservative' jurists on the federal bench, and not one generally thought to be particularly soft on criminal defendants."

Post continued his assessment as follows: "The court held that the Michigan statute was *punishing* registrants, and could not therefore be applied to persons convicted of the underlying sex offence *prior* to its enactment." The court did look at five factors—non-dispositive guideposts—to make the determination it reached.

"(1) Does the law inflict what has been regarded in our history and traditions as punishment? (2) Does it impose an affirmative disability or restrains? (3) Does it promote the traditional aims of punishment? (4) Does it have a rational connection to a non-punitive purpose? (5) Is it excessive with respect to this purpose?"

His analysis also looked at all five factors and found that all DID weigh in favor of a finding that the Michigan SORA was indeed punitive. The Act imposed serious—even life-changing—disabilities and restraints on those subject to its prohibitions.

Post concludes his own argument as follows: "The court's decision does not affect *non*-retroactive application of the statutory requirements, it does appear to rather clearly point the way to a broader invalidation. Now that the court has held that the requirements imposed indeed constitute *punishment,* the Ex Post Facto Clause protects only against retroactive imposition of that punishment; but the Due Process and Equal Protection Clauses protect against arbitrary impositions of that punishment on anyone, and the court's subsidiary holding here—that the requirements bear no rational relation to the law's stated purpose, and that the state had no evidence that they do any good at all—may well mean that they contravene those broader protections against arbitrary and oppressive government action."

Sex Offender Laws Now Challenged

An article on August 11, 2014 for *Jurisprudence* by Matt Mellema, Chanakya Sethi, and Jane Shim was given the headline: "Sex Offender Laws Have Gone Too Far—Our draconian policies about sex offences reflect our ignorance of them." On October 22, 1989, 11-year-old Jacob Wetterling was kidnapped while biking home from a convenience store. "Nearly 25 years ago, Jacob remains missing and the identity of his kidnapper is unknown."

His mother led the fight for stronger laws and ways of letting parents and other citizens be aware of who was a sex offender and where they were living. The Jacob Wetterling Crimes Against Children and Sexually Violent Offender Registration Act was signed by President Bill Clinton in 1994.

Using federal dollars to states, they were pushed to develop a registry.

Megan's Law, was enacted in 1996 and in 2006 the Sex Offender Registration and Notification Act was passed. Both said that anyone convicted of such a crime had to be registered and numerous small but significant "facts" about the offender had to be added to the record. The result was simple and awful—with now more than 750,000 persons being listed.

But now raising major questions about them is, among others, Patty Wetterling, mother of still-missing Jacob. *She says*: "We need to know what science can tell us about the nature of sex offenders." For example we now know that the odds of a an offender repeating his offense is very low. We now also know that strangers were the most likely to offend but now it is much more likely to be a person already known to the child.

For example, recidivism, was found to be very low and much, much less than the public's view. It is also known that a child is much more likely to be approached by a family member or someone else known to the family. Again, this is in contrast to what people believe to be true.

Mrs. Wetterling is now seeking help in making the actual facts about the problems more commonly known by people. Suggestions were given to go to such sources as Human Rights Watch, the American Bar Association, and the Government Accountability Office.

Efforts to Change Offender Registration Date Back Years

"Albuquerque, NM: A national conference headed to Albuguerque aims to reform or soften current sex offender laws and the registry." A local man had been convicted of sexual assault in Texas in 1987. "My conviction was over 25 years ago..and I served my sentence over 15 years ago. And yet I'm still being punished, and my family is still being punished." This lead was in a story on August 29, 2012, KOTA.com.

Thus his story is just one of the many similar forces behind a national conference in Albuquerque which will be the fourth annual Reform Sexual Offender National Conference. It will feature lawyers, judges, and therapists. Both the current governor and attorney general for NM say they will oppose any weakening of the current state laws.

"RSOL: Reform Sex Offender Laws: Solid Facts, Prevention, Restoration, Civil Liberty, Human Dignity" was the lead for an April 2013 story by the Webmaster for the RSOL blog. The story leads with many key quotes such as, "Victims first, sex offenders second," and "How can anyone care about the rights of sex offenders? The rights of children come first." Obviously, there remains distinct opposition to changes in the punishment of sex offenders.

"In a recently released report, this statement, originally found in Criminal Justice and Behavior (May 2010 37:477-481) was used: sex offender policies are often inconsistent with empirical evidence about sex offender risks: recidivism, reintegration and supervision....Legislators cite the news media and the views of their constituents—not research evidence—as their primary sources of information about sex offenses and offenders."

Chanakya Sethl writing for the Jurisprudence blog on August 12, 2014, used the following headline for her article, "The Ridiculous Laws That Put People on the Sex Offender List." Included in this posting were three maps that would show that people had been registered as sex offenders for consensual teenage sex, peeing in public, and prostitution."

The story of a young man of 18 and his girlfriend of 14 made a decision to have sex. This meant that he could have been charged with statutory rape but was able to bargain it down but the Registry continued. They separated, but then reconnected, were married but could no longer live happily ever after—he was registered.

He says he lost 17 jobs because of his status. He could not attend his sons' ball games or his daughter's dance recitals. "I wish I could take it back. Once we got back together I realized how detrimental being registered was to him and them." Brenda Jones, executive Director of Reform Sex Offender Laws, a volunteer advocacy group said, "But lawmakers aren't paying attention, and we as constituents are not aware."

Map I showed at least 29/50 states can charge underage teens for having consensual sex. Map II showed at least 12/50 states can demand registry for peeing in public. Map III showed that at least 6/50 can use prostitution-related offenses as grounds for registry. Some changes are still very much needed as being on the registry can become a lifelong journey for former 'violaters' now out and in the public where possible.

It is this 'lifelong' impact of our current punishment process that is at issue. It is this denial of being able to find adequate housing, this ability to be an active participating parent that attends a child's sports and music events, and this ability to become an active adult in the local society that are too often still denied by current 'registration' laws. <u>And this is wrong!</u>

CHAPTER 14

Prison Sentences (Death, Isolation, etc.)

How do we know when, if ever, to support a death penalty sentence for a person? This is the most significant action that a state can take in bringing retribution to an individual. With dozens of cases having been "re-opened" based on additional testimony and/or new evidence being made available, confidence in our American 'justice for all' system has been changing and quite rapidly. Suddenly many more death cases are once again in the public eye.

The Slow Demise of Capital Punishment

The Monday, December 30, 2013 *The New York Times,* editorial also had a second sub-headline which read: "Just 2 percent of counties in the United States are responsible for all death sentences." The editorial began as follows: "More states are coming to recognize that the death penalty is arbitrary, racially biased, and prone to catastrophic error." The opening paragraph then went on to point out that even if it still exists as a possibility, many other places are also NOT using it in practice.

"As it becomes less frequent, the death penalty also becomes more limited to an extremely small slice of the country, and therefore all the more arbitrary in its application. All 80 death sentences in 2013 came from only about 2 percent of counties in the entire country, and all 39 executions---more than half occurred in Texas and Florida---took place in about 1 percent of all counties."

With public support for the death penalty at the lowest level in four decades there is less argument in favor of it. Add to that the "hundreds of exonerations based on DNA testing" the public's confidence in this capital punishment is disappearing. But this does little to give hope to the 3,100 people still sitting on death row in all types of prisons in our nation.

The Death Penalty Endgame

Ever since 1976 when the court allowed executions to resume after its 4 year moratorium, the debate and discussion has again been resumed. Since then 1,423 people have been put to death according to this *The New York Times* January 1, 2016 editorial. Since a high of about 80 percent of Americans supporting the death penalty in the 1980s, that level have dropped to about 60 percent now and when given an option of death vs. life without parole—fell to only 50 percent still in support. In some cases, *voter*s have changed state laws regarding the death penalty.

"In the past 14 years alone, the Supreme Court has barred the execution of several categories of people: minors, the intellectually disabled, and those convicted of a crime other than murder." In the last example, Justice Anthony Kennedy wrote for the court, "When the law punishes by death, it risks its own sudden descent into brutality, transgressing the constitutional commitment to decency and restraint."

Justice Stephen Breyer's dissent argued that the death penalty was "unreliable, arbitrary, and racially discriminatory." He stated that in instead of patching up the holes in case after case, we should make a definitive ruling because the entire capital punishment "most likely violates the Eighth Amendment." Any such decisions, even their discussions, are steps in the right direction for change.

"Race and the Death Penalty in Texas," was the headline for an editorial in *The New York Times* on April 3, 2016. Because Mr. Duane Buck's case was held in Harris County Texas (Houston), several other factors rise to the surface. Mr. Buck is Black. "In a seven-year period that included Mr. Buck's trial, Harris County prosecutors were more than three times as likely to seek the death penalty against a black defendant as against a white one. Over the past dozen years, every new death sentence in the county has been imposed on a man of color."

Court Overturns Death Sentence

Adam Liptak writing in the *Dayton Daily News* on Wednesday, June 1, 2016 under a category heading of Capital Cases. The article headline was, "Supreme Court overturns death sentence...In 2nd case, justices reject challenge to death penalty." Just a day before the Court rejected a broad constitutional challenge to capital punishment from Louisiana yet reversed a death sentence from Arizona.

In the Louisiana case the Court followed its own past practice and refused to deal with the constitutional issue directly while still refusing to overturn this case of a man who was only 18 with an IQ of 74. But in the second case they overturned the conviction of Shawn P. Lynch because **no one** had been willing to make the point that there was an alternative sentence of life in prison with no chance for parole. Failure to even acknowledge alternatives to death is also unconstitutional seems to be a dramatic step forward in limiting the use of the death penalty.

Pfizer Blocks Use of Its Drugs

Erik Echolm writing for *The New York Times* on May 14, 2016 brought forth a major set- back to the use of Pfizer's lethal drugs as having any part in the chemical cookbook involved in death by injection. Many other companies had also prohibited the use of their drugs for such a purpose and this was a type of last straw. Pfizer's drug was the last open-market source of lethal drugs and it was now closed.

"The pharmaceutical giant Pfizer announced Friday that it has imposed sweeping controls on the distribution of its products to ensure that none will be used in lethal injections, a step that closes off the last remaining open-market source of drugs used in executions." This action now closes the marketing of such drugs as has already been done by another

20 U.S. and European drug companies. Corporate fear of bad public relations or good awareness of not wanting to be associated with bad practice have come forward to help with more justice.

This now has some states talking about reinstituting the electric chair, or the firing squad, or the gas chamber. But the later choice would still have its own set of problems. Given that states must also meet full disclosure of all purchases, they now have still another problem.

Using local U.S. compounding sites also raises major questions of transparency and quality of the items being purchased. "States are now shrouding in secrecy aspects of what should be the most transparent government activity," said Ty Albert of the University of California Berkley School of Law.

Such surveys of government also fails to meet the government openness laws and practices. Failure to follow what increasingly the public is demanding can be a major risk and the drug companies do not want to be seen as being involved in what the public finds distasteful or wrong.

Supreme Court Takes 2 New Cases

The *Christian Science Monitor*'s article for its June 20, 2016 issue indicated in its sub-headline that "Justices will skirt primary question of constitutionality." Staff writer, Henry Glass says that both cases are from Texas and will NOT look at how defendants are treated while on death row. This is still likely to bring forth much new data into the court system.

Solitary confinement may well have its own very separate place in the future.

Mr. Duane Buck's case will force the court to examine the role of race in the judicial system closely. Mr. Bobbie Moore's case also brings into the open the **solitary confinement** issue. Glass writes, "He's been held in solitary confinement nearly 23 hours a day for the past 15 years---in cells described by some of **'incubators of psychoses'**—but the court has declined to consider whether his confinement violates the Eighth Amendment's prohibition against cruel and unusual punishment."

The New York Times editorial on October 24, 2016 looked at the national attitude toward capital punishment via its headline, "The Death Penalty, Nearing Its End." This polling result was found to be encouraging for those who fight the use of this penalty by the courts.

It was also supportive of the element of the public that increasingly is favoring judicial reform.

New Polls/Studies

A new poll by Gallup which reported, "Support for the death penalty in the United States is at its lowest level since November, 1972. The *Death Penalty Information Center (DPIC)* has also stated that two new studies reported: "Death Penalty Adversely Affects Families of Victims and Defendants." It cited a University of Minnesota study which showed that only 2.5 percent of victim families/friends felt that the execution helped them achieving closure while 20.5 percent said it offered no help at all.

Another recent posting by the DPIC was on October 20, 2016. It dealt with the number of executions by Harris County (Texas, Houston). The county "leads the nation in executions…Although the 10 new death sentences imposed in Harris County since 2010 are more than were imposed by 99.5 percent of U.S. counties, they are significantly fewer than the 53 death sentences that were handed down in Harris in 1998-2003 and the 16 from 2004-2009.

"The 2016 Kinder Institute survey of Houston residents showed that just 27% prefer the death penalty over life sentences for those convicted of first-degree murder." Even though these numbers represent a major decline, they do not address the "systemic problems of prosecutorial misconduct, inadequate representation, and racial bias that still persist." K. S., "a prosecutor who obtained 19 death sentences was found by a Texas court to have committed 36 instances of misconduct in a single murder case." The misconduct by prosecutors cannot be allowed to take lives in the process of the errors made.

The Death Penalty Information Center (DPIC) also reported on October 18, 2016 that the Lincoln, NE *Journal Star* editorial was very explicit in its editorial urging Nebraska *voters* to end the State's Death Penalty on November 8, 2016. "Saying that the death penalty is too fallible to endure" the editorial further "urged Nebraskans to retain (keep) the legislature's death penalty repeal bill."

The paper further reported on the errors that have occurred right here in the state. The famous case of the Beatrice 6 was overturned when years later, DNA results fully exonerated the six and now the county of Gage was left with finding $28.1

million in damages to be paid to these men. The *Omaha World-Herald* has run a 3-part series on the whole issue thus far.

"In California, which hasn't executed anyone since 2006 even though more than 740 inmates sit on death row, voters will decide in November whether to eliminate capital punishment for good," reported *The New York Times.*

Solitary Confinement

"Solitary confinement of prisoners goes by a number of names—isolation, SHU (special housing units), administrative segregation, supermax prisons, the hole, MCU (management control units), CMU (communications management units), STGMU (security threat group management units), voluntary or involuntary protective custody, special needs units, or permanent lockdown," led the undated article by the *American Friends Service Committee (AFSC).* Such units exist throughout the prison system although such solitary confinement conditions vary from state to state and among correctional facilities, systematic policies and conditions include:

- "Confinement behind a solid steel door for 22 to 24 hours a day
- Severely limited contact with other human beings
- Infrequent phone calls and rare non-contact family visits
- Extremely limited access to rehabilitative or educational programming

- Grossly inadequate medical and mental health treatment
- Restricted reading material and personal property
- Physical torture such as hog-tying, restraint chairs, forced cell extraction
- 'No-touch torture' such as sensory deprivation, permanent bright lighting, extreme temperatures, and forced insomnia
- Chemical torture, such as stun grenades and stun guns
- Sexual intimidation and other forms of brutality and humiliation"

Nearly every state has some form of the above to use in its own version of solitary confinement within its prison systems. BUT there is no federal system for reporting such use or how many people are housed in such systems. "Prisoners are often confined for months or even years, with some spending more than 25 years in such segregated prison settings. As with the overall prison population, people of color are disproportionately represented in isolation units."

This issue of extended amount of time being spent in such closed confinement is at the heart of the "cruel and unusual punishment" constitutional issue now being raised. It is an essential issue in judicial reform and must be given close attention by all parties.

The AFSC report raises a most pertinent and significant question, "How does long-term solitary confinement affect a person?" It then sites numerous studies which have documented the harmful psychological effects of long-term solitary confinement which can produce these types of debilitating symptoms, such as:

- "Visual and auditory hallucinations
- Hypersensitivity to noise and touch
- Insomnia and paranoia
- Uncontrollable feelings of rage and fear
- Distortions of time and perception
- Increased risk of suicide
- Post-traumatic stress disorder (PTSD)"

"If a person isn't mentally ill when entering an isolation unit, by the time they are released, their mental health has been severely compromised. Many prisoners are released directly to the streets after spending years in isolation. Because of this, long-term solitary confinement goes beyond a problem of prison conditions, to pose a formidable public safety and community health problem."

In May 2015 the VERA Institute of Justice Center on Sentencing and Corrections issued its report. The title, "Solitary Confinement: Common Misconceptions and Emerging Safe Alternatives," gives many clues as to this organization's views of what has been such a major problem. Their report includes the following words: "Evidence mounts that solitary confinement produces many unwanted and harmful outcomes—for the mental and physical health of those placed in isolation, for the public safety of the communities to which most will return, and for the corrections budgets of jurisdictions that rely on the practice for facility safety." The report is available via *cherrman@vera.org*.

The New York Times article of August 3, 2015 by Erica Goode was headlined, "Solitary Confinement: Punished for Life." Goode describes a major study by Dr. Craig Haney, a social psychologist, who worked with inmates at Pelican Bay State Prison, California's toughest penal institution. His results could be summarized in the following words:

"Sealed for years in a hermetic environment—one inmate likened the prison's solitary confinement unit to 'a weapons lab or a place for human experiments'—prisoners recounted struggling daily to maintain their sanity. They spoke of longing to catch sight of a tree or a bird. Many responded to their isolation by shutting down their emotions and withdrawing even further, shunning even the meager human conversation and company they were afforded."

It is very clear that Solitary Confinement is a key part of the prison life that must be changed in both state and federal prisons. Our society must be on the lookout for differing ways of dealing with humans. This issue has too many long-lasting detriments that are turning humans into mental-cases. We need to address this part of incarceration whether it is in prison or jail, local or federal as part of a real Justice for All effort.

CHAPTER 15

Reforms for the Judicial System

While a number of suggested changes and reforms have been included within the many previous chapters of this book, they were not designed to serve to meet the many changes needed. This chapter will be much longer and contain dozens of good practices already in operation at places throughout the justice system but could be doing much more good if similar use were found all over the system.

I will not attempt to follow the chapter designations but rather just highlight *some* of the many reforms and new practices now in place. My goal is for you to leave this pre-election chapter with a sense of the excellent reforms now in place and a desire to make sure that they are able to be continued in 2018 and beyond.

But first let me summarize the five prime areas of juvenile and criminal justice reforms for which the Southern Poverty Law Center (SPLC) is currently working. These brief statements will provide the readers with a set of guidelines against which to measure the many real efforts also reported within in this chapter.

"We're (SPLC) working to reform juvenile and criminal justice systems so they operate fairly and equitably; to ensure the dignity and humanity of those interacting with these systems; and to reduce the prison population. We're using litigation and advocacy to help end the era of mass incarceration, to root out racial discrimination in the system, and to ensure humane, constitutional standards for prisoners:

- Reforming policies that lead to the incarceration of children and teens for minor crimes and school-related offenses;
- Working to transform a juvenile system that subjects children to abuse and neglect without providing necessary medical, mental health, educational and rehabilitative services;
- Ensuring that prisoners are not subjected to unconstitutional, inhumane conditions and that they receive proper medical and mental health care;
- Seeking to stop the prosecution of children in the adult criminal justice system and their incarceration in adult prisons and jails;
- Advocating for rational policies and laws that keep communities safe while vastly shrinking the prison population and reducing the social and economic impact of mass incarceration on vulnerable communities." (9-22-2016)

Each of these is vital for our justice system to provide justice for all from youth to adult, from females to males, from long-time citizens to recent immigrants, and from urban to rural folks. We need to work for all of them. Being aware of key policy elements is an integral value in this process.

Ten Policy Solutions

Kevin Mathews writing on August 24, 2015 presents a list of solutions with very clear policy proposals to bring 'life' to what has been on the minds of those working in the Black Lives Matter movement. What follows is his brief description of what is needed in order to bring a significant change in the law enforcement-community relations worlds of America. Kevin is a contributor to Care2.com. The 10 Policy Solutions are presented below.

1. **End Broken Windows Policing**
2. **Community Oversight**
3. **Limit Use of Force**
4. **Independently Investigate & Prosecute**
5. **Community Representation**
6. **Body Cameras/Film the Police**
7. **Training**
8. **End For–Profit Policing**
9. **Demilitarization**
10. **Fair Police Union Contracts**

These broad-based categories open up much for concrete targeting of changes that can do much to bring about constructive and positive changes to our judicial systems for juveniles and for adults. For example, stop police emphasis on such simple actions as having a broken window in your car, house, or business or for breaking a window. Abolish laws which have police helping to pad the budget of the city via parking or turning violations. The use of more body cameras will not only help people to trust, but will help the police from 'misbehaving' as well.

The American Bar Association's Rule of Law Initiative (ABA ROLI) has been working to help our own system of judicial process from law enforcement through trials and then judgments. Their November 8, 2016 Judicial Reform document sets forth their own list of key actions needed with five significant areas for reform. "ABA ROLI believes that an independent, accountable, effective judiciary is a central pillar of the rule of law. With this in mind, we offer expert assistance in and provide resources for:

- Conducting assessments of judicial reform efforts
- Facilitating dialogue on judicial reform and independence
- Promoting education and training for judges and court personnel
- Improving judicial ethics and accountability
- Strengthening court administration, efficiency and transparency."

Such help is readily available from ABA ROLI for all levels of government and might well be able to provide real assistance in moving forward with judicial and justice system reform.

Training, Training, Training

Diana Nelson Jones wrote the article, "For Inmates, training dogs a bonus: Program also make shelter canines more adoptable," for the *Pittsburgh Post Gazette.* Printed on June 7, 2016, she tells the story of a five-year relationship with Strayhaven Animal Shelter and the SCI Mercer, PA. The prison has taken 122 dogs and all but one have been adopted even though many came in with behavioral issues. But their basic personalities came through with the guidance and help of the prisoners who trained them.

Many prisons nation-wide have similar programs under various names but do use prisoners to train dogs for different skills including service to people with special needs. Corrections staff members say that the prisoners also show their basic personalities for their own good. Such training is most worthwhile according to prison authorities.

Holly Zachariah writing for the *Columbus Dispatch* on January 2, 2016 about a program which helped inmates and felines as the prisoners prepared kittens and cats for adoption. At the Madison Correctional Institution the 10 prisoners are a part of the "foster cat program." Fifteen men are on the waiting list for a chance to take part!

The prisoners grow in their own care as they work with the cats and this is what has such a waiting list. There are many more cats available than the institution has the ability to provide the adult care-giver for. More space and more funds would enable even more men to also benefit.

Training Staff: The June 24, 2016 issue of *Time* carried an article by Jose Sanburn of Burien, WA entitled, "POLICING Restoring order to the rule of law." The story begins in a drab second-floor classroom with two dozen cops being encouraged to talk about themselves. Slowly they do begin to open up and to relate to the efforts.

"This reminds us of why we are doing our job." says one of the men. They have borrowed so much from the military that it has become too much of the key to so much of their interactions they seem to be saying now. Sue Rahr has been put in charge of the Police Academy now and this is what she is trying to accomplish.

"The message is that not everything ends in an arrest. Most people can be de-escalated. Not all of them, but unless you give them the opportunity, you're not going to know." Rahr continues, "Failure to comply does not necessarily indicate resistance." But too many police leaders and members do not buy her message. Police unions have been able to develop very tight union contracts which keep tight control of hiring, firing, disciplining, and other key factors.

Rahr concludes the article with these words, "It's a little bit ironic that this building used to be a church…It's much easier to get the officers in the frame of mind of 'I'm serving a higher purpose' here." The training like this is a very fundamental key to changing and reforming the justice system.

Training Prisoners: Mark Reiter wrote for the *Toledo Blade* and his article posted on June 25, 2016. It carried a very revealing headline: "Program helps prison inmates reinvent lives: People 'come out of this class with a plan.'" Elmer Yeary is quoted as saying, "My life was a mess. Now, I am working on getting my own housing. I want to go to school."

He was one of the members in the 11-week training course which included a two-hour-30-minute class twice a week. He feels that the efforts for him to help himself were essential. Judge Timothy Kuhlman of the Toledo Municipal Court summed it up as follows:

"We do all sorts of things to try to help people not return to jail. That is our goal. We want people to come back to community to have successful lives." he said.

Prisoner Vocational Village: David Eggert writing for the Associated Press in October 16, 2016 carried the following headline in the *Dayton Daily News.* It read: "Mich. Trains inmates for jobs in 'vocational village'; State aims to keep freed prisoners from coming back." Michigan has been among the best states in reducing its prison population except for the return of many back into the prison system.

"Now Michigan is trying to stop the boomerang effect with a new program that removes soon-to-be-released inmates from the general population and assigns them to an exclusive 'vocational village' for job training. The idea is to send them out through the prison gates with marketable skills that lead to a stable job, the kind that will keep them out of trouble long term."

They are separated from the main prison population by having them up and in classes where they work on acquiring the readiness skills and attitudes needed to hold a job. The prisoners are helped to value the work habits such as giving a full day's work which can be essential to success in the work world. Such skills as carpentry, welding, building, etc. are among the ones being stressed in this program.

Chris Chavanne is a third time inmate for having robbed a bank at age 16. Now he has landed a construction job upon his next release. He said, "I feel like I've learned enough to stay the heck out of here and go on to be successful. I do feel more equipped and more confident to do something better than what I was doing."

The 'feds' are also making some changes. After cutting its prison education program, the staff and leadership at the Elkton (OH) federal low-level prison is now seeming to want to make several programs eligible for inmates. HVAC, Electronics, Plumbing, Food Services, and Construction are now open for select inmates to use. They seem to now see the value of them for their best prisoners.

Women inmates also have needs. Cara Tabachnick writing for the July 20, 2015 issue of the *Christian Science Monitor* quoted Georgia Lerner executive director of the Women's Prison Association as follows: "If we want to stop women [ex-convicts] from returning to prison, we have to do things differently." Tanya Jisa's story moves ahead with the goal just expressed as she has moved to bring the needy ex-inmates to become an integral part of her new home farm raising essential products for needy people in and around Graham, NC.

Located not far from the 'golden triangle' (Research Triangle) of North Carolina where many colleges are located, she started to tell farmers and others at the local markets about her idea for a farm where women prisoners could live and work. "People responded positively and in the winter of 2007 she held focus groups with people returning from prison." This led to the basic structure of Benevolence Farm.

Architectural students from a local university helped design a needed building and then the construction of it. Others worked with the clearing of the land. Still others provided guidance on the marketing. Bottom line, the farm was created and has become a local living legend for the good of ex-inmates who see it as their new home! One stated it this way: "When you get back into society after being incarcerated you feel worthless...On the farm it's just me, God, and the plants. This will give me time to think, and maybe I can get my life back on track."

ALL of the above items are just examples of how education of prisoners has been changed for the positive. These inmates are much more likely to be able to become a positive part of the society they re-enter upon release.

Feds to Get Involved

Eric Lichtblau of the *New York Times* on Saturday, October 15, 2016 in an article in the *Dayton Daily News* called major attention to the Feds being ready to track the use of force by police in the United States. Attorney General Loretta Lynch has said that collection of data will start early next year. "I can't believe two years ago into this crisis that we're still having conversations about data, said Kanya Bennet, a lawyer in Washington for the American Civil Liberties Union, which met with the Justice Department to discuss the plan."

James Comey (FBI Director) told lawmakers a year ago that it was "embarrassing that the news media could produce better data than his own agency on such an important issue. We can't have an informed discussion because we don't have data." He provided some examples and then summarized, "And that's a very bad place to be!"

Under the Justice Department plan the FBI is to begin a pilot program early next year to assemble data on the use of force by about 178,000 agents in the federal government agencies including the FBI, itself. This should help us very quickly.

Police Chiefs Association Apologizes to U.S.

On October 19, 2016 the *USA TODAY,* carried a very significant story by John Bacon with headline: "Cop apologizes for minority 'mistreatment'; Head of police chiefs' group says officers must build trust." The story then continues with this key initial paragraph. "An apology for the role police officers played in society's historical mistreatment of communities of color" by the president of the International Association of Chiefs of Police (IACP), Terrance Cunningham at their annual conference.

He continued, "The first step in this process is for law enforcement and the IACP to acknowledge and apologize for the actions of the past and the role that our profession has played in society's historical mistreatment of communities of color. At the same time, those who denounce the police must also acknowledge that today's officers are not to blame for the injustices of the past.

In a separate article on this same event, Tom Jackman writing for the *Washington Post* on October 18, 2016, wrote that Cunningham had cited laws enacted by state and federal governments which "have required police officers to perform many unpalatable tasks…while this is no longer the case, the dark side of our shared history has created a multigenerational—almost inherited—mistrust between communities of color and their own law enforcement agencies."

Jeffery Robinson of the ACLU saluted Cunningham's statement in these words: "It seems to me that this is a very significant admission and a very significant acknowledgement of what much of America has known for some time about the historical relationship between police and communities of color…And I think it's a necessary first step to them trying to change these relationships."

Child (7) Tries to Sell Toy for Food

The local Ohio police system got a call from its dispatcher that a child was near the CVS store trying to sell his stuffed toy so that he could buy some food. This started a very positive set of events that brought a solution to a problem and honor to all city staff involved. Franklin, OH is a small city located just south of Dayton, OH and the press featured the story on Saturday, August 13, 2016 with the sub-headlne: "Officer gets child food; child, siblings removed from home." Ed Richter wrote this early story for the *Dayton Daily News.*

Officer Steve Dunham went to the store and found the boy with his stuffed animal. He said he had not had any food for days. Immediately, the officer took the boy across the street to a Subway and solved the prime need for food before taking him to the police station. Two other officers, Amanda Myers and Kyle O'Neal went to the boy's home where they found his siblings living in a home full of garbage, cat urine, and liquor bottles. All five of the children were then placed with relatives and the parents arrested for child endangering.

Several months later local TV stations featured a story of the local City Council honoring the officers and dispatcher involved for their prompt actions in leading to the successful solution for this case. The small boy's attempt to solve his basic problem had been recognized and the 'system' had responded with care and concern to solve the problem. The press, both paper and TV, played a part in this case in the way in which it was aired and given public attention.

Firefighters Take Control of School Shooting Scene

An Associated Press story by Kate Brumback and Jay Reeves on September 30, 2016 carried a sub-headline as follows: "Chief aided critically hurt child, volunteer subdued the suspect." When the chief and a volunteer firefighter rolled up to an elementary school shooting, what they did find led them to take actions that would cause their small community of Townville, SC to hail them as heroes.

Since they were the very first responders to arrive at the scene, they quickly engaged in the "preserve and protect" part of their profession. "Within minutes they performed actions...one went inside to help treat the wounded and the other found and subdued the shooter." The shooter never made it inside the school building although he shot and wounded several people.

"This was more than just another call to us. This incident occurred in the school where our children and the children of the community attend," Fire Chief Billy McAdams said. The Chief tended to those injured, especially Jacob Hall, age 6, and firefighter Jamie Brock searched for and found the shooter whom he subdued until police had arrived.

That such actions by "other" first responders makes such news and is given such publicity clearly helps send a message to the public. The message also is read by law enforcement members throughout this nation and hopefully makes a difference.

Policing's Sci-fi Future Is Near

The *Christian Science Monitor* of August 15-22, 2016 included this story by Jessica Mendoza about a Sacramento, CA surveillance hub raises hope and concerns. Like New York, Houston, Miami, and other places, now Sacramento has what is being called, "real-time crime center." "The idea is that by consolidating information on criminal activity would make police more effective." A central location "from which officers could monitor all their surveillance technologies." This process would help police become more accountable and responsible and transparent as they carry out their ordinary day-to-day duties.

BUT "the technology raises other issues. Already concerned about POD's privacy advocates are troubled by the prospect of centralizing law-enforcement data, especially in a post 9-11 world where data are being shared more widely across federal, state, and local lines. A backlash is rising." Some critics say that type of predictive policing reinforces racial profiling and violates civil liberties with little accountability. BUT "privacy advocates have praised the ordinance." The concept of better policing merits such moves but caution also should prevail.

William J. Bratton, commissioner of the New York City Police Department and one of the most widely recognized names in American law enforcement has just announced his retirement. But his quote is significant. He said, "Policing is never done; it's always unfinished business. The issues that we're facing now are going to require years to resolve." *Christian Science Monitor,* August 15-22, 2016.

Racial Profiling in Preschool

The *New York Times* editorial on Sunday, October 9, 2016 led with these words: "That black adolescents receive harsher disciplinary punishments at school than their white peers for the same offenses is troubling enough. But federal data showing that even at the preschool level black students are nearly four times as likely to be suspended as their white peers is especially shocking." The preschool-to-prison pipeline begins VERY early in the career of our children it seems.

"Chief among these mechanisms, according to a new report from the Yale University's Child Study Center, are racial preconceptions that shape the way the teachers view black boys in particular. These preconceptions were found to exist in black as well as white preschool teachers."

Now that such problems DO exist and that we KNOW impact of them on the futures of our children, we must do something about it. Some will doubt the truth of this and others will work to find ways to ignore it, BUT well-informed educators will find ways to counter such preconceptions and to take on one more problem. This is now a part of the planning on how to break the famous 'pipeline'!

Bringing Faiths Together in Women's Prison

A lengthy article for the *Columbus Dispatch* written by JoAnna Viviano and published on October 8, 2016 in the *Dayton Daily News* carried the following headline: "Program brings faiths together at women's prison." When Kellie Hurley entered the gates of the Ohio Reformatory for Women six years ago, she made a very major choice to change both her own thinking and actions. Now she will be one of the first inmates to take part in the Horizon Prison Initiative.

This program places the women of various backgrounds, faiths, etc. into family-like units. They then begin to explore their beliefs, spirituality, and delve into previous traumas while also learning new skills. They are ages 20 to 73, Catholic and Protestant, Jewish and Buddhist, Mormon and Jehovah's Witness, Unitarian Universalist, Wiccan and Native American. Yes! Very diverse very intentionally! It is on this type of base that the Horizon plan is able to function most effectively.

Retired United Methodist Church Bishop C. Joseph Sprague is the President of the Horizon board. His comments to the group at its opening event included these comments. "What Horizon is about is not putting a shine on anyone. That is a misuse of people. It's one of the reasons seven out of 10 inmates in the U. S. return to jail. We're talking about systemic transformation, getting down here because your souls are sick, and we don't handle them as if they are 'things'."

The inmates participate for 10 months performing regular prison duties and keeping regular prison schedules while doing their Horizon work in the evenings. "Funds that used to come from the state budget; now they come from the civil-litigation fund in the state attorney general's office and from donors." This year half of the needed dollars were covered by national leaders of the Unitarian Universalist Association.

Warden Ronette Burkes had wanted this program for years. "When you learn about other cultures, about other religions, about others' beliefs—you are often times more tolerant." Thus she is glad to have the Horizon Program in her prison helping her inmates prepare to live in harmony when they leave here!

Building Bridges—Youth and Police

Mary McCarty wrote a lengthy article on November 23, 2016 for the *Dayton Daily News* in which she focused on a "Crusader builds a bridge between youth, police." This was on page one but the headline on A10 said, "Organizer helps build youth, police understanding" with a sub-headline, "Police and Youth Together program makes a difference."

"Mary E. Tyler, executive director for the National Conference for Community and Justice of Greater Dayton stands up against racism…(she) doesn't just talk about improving relationships between police and community, she works every day to make it happen…And she knows the best place to start: with young people."

"We are changing the perception that young people (ages 10-12) have about law enforcement and it's a two-way change of perspective---officers are interacting and connecting with young people," Tyler said. She leads the summer program which involves a week-long summer camp that "is the beginning of relationships that can stretch on for years." Both the children and the police come from many areas of the community. The "fun camp with a serious message" is designed to present serious messages such as confronting bullies, how to report a crime, and respecting authority.

CASA—Great Program for Foster Kids

I almost forgot about this organization, Court Appointed Special Advocate, even though I was a full member for close to a decade. CASAs are fully trained in 30 hours of class time and then via regular training throughout the year via the juvenile court staff. These volunteers are made up of lawyers and ordinary citizens who agree to serve one or two youth who have been placed in "foster homes" as their own personal legal representative.

Char Williams, a CASA in Texas, wrote a short article for the December 12, 2016 issue of the *Christian Science Monitor.* Her training was for children who had been abused or neglected. Many have the potential for becoming a part of the prison system if not carefully guarded and have this advocate. As an official court officer in each case, the CASA is able to sit in on all Special Education hearings, obtain all medical records, talk to school leaders, church leaders, and all relevant family members.

"While we are not legal experts," says Williams, "we are the voice of the children. We learn about the situation that led to the child's removal from the home and about the particular challenges the child is facing and we recommend to the Judge what is best for that individual child." The CASA prepares a formal report and then attends court to serve as a witness to help explain any questions the Judge may have.

My own experience included very small new born to families of multiple children ranging from grade 1 to grade 10. I had to fight the Childrens' Services (only one time) but also to work closely with them as much as possible. Our goal was always to prevent full incarceration whenever possible and to help the child obtain a full diploma. This is one youth program that should be found in all states and county offices. I strongly support this program as some of these children had already been or could have been in juvenile court and on the road to moving to prison later.

County Attorney Calls for Good Start in School

David Parish felt that he needed to speak out so he wrote a letter to the editor of the *Omaha World-Herald* and saw his work published October 9, 2016. He wrote, "My first job as county attorney (for Otoe County, Nebraska City) is to uphold the law and put away those who are an immediate threat to public safety. But I know from experience and research that we can't arrest our way out of the crime problem. We must also focus on what works to prevent crime."

He is arguing for helping the kids by making sure that they get off to a good start in life by a good education prior to starting school and then continuing it on through their school career. He along with 100 other law enforcement leaders in Nebraska have joined together to support **Fight Crime: Invest in Kids**---a non-profit organization focused on "protecting public safety by promoting solutions that steer kids away from crime."

He adds that, "When our kids have these early learning opportunities, they are more likely to build critical skills that lay the foundation for future academic success and will make it less likely that they will eventually drop out." It did my heart good to read such strong support for quality early childhood education from a leading county official.

Strengthening the Spirit of Inmates via Books

Husna Haq's short article in the October 17, 2016 issue of the *Christian Science Monitor* opens up a number of aspects of this process. "It may not be cruel, but there's an unusual punishment being practiced in some prisons across the United States…reading."

"At least some jails, judges, and yes, literature professors around the world tend to agree. In fact there are many organizations that promote reading as remediation, especially for young or petty criminals including Changing Lives Through Literature (CLTL), a program cofounded in 1991 by Robert Waxler, a professor of English…and later expanded throughout the world and now in the U.S."

Through programs such as this one, thousands of offenders across the country have been placed in a rehabilitation reading program as an alternative to prison. Prisoners are placed in groups where they read and discuss extensively themes which relate to their own offenses. Themes of anger, love, tolerance, empathy and liberty are samples.

A year-long study of such programs has shown them to have lasting value especially as the prisoners are released for return to society. At least it has been a much less expensive and much more beneficial program than what is typically found (or missing totally) in our nation's prisons.

Vets Being Trained to Be "HERO" (Fight Child Porn)

Anna Mulrine's major article in the July 20, 2015 issue of the *Christian Science Monitor* presents in good detail the work of wounded war vets now a part of the Human Exploitation Rescue Operative (HERO) Corps in Washington. "After being all but eradicated in the U.S. in the 1980s, child pornography has exploded in the Digital Age. In fighting it, some veterans—already trained to be tenacious and to cope with disturbing images—say they have found a new way to serve their country."

Their work now opens a new front in the growing war against child predators. Their work has enabled them to help authorities to prosecute the predators and to locate the victims of such material. In the first years of HERO, the vets helped whittle down a two-year backlog and to speed up the ability to bring perpetrators to justice.

One vet, Justin Gaertner, participated in a recent bust that helped take down a child pornography ring with 130 victims and 28,000 images that the National Center for Missing & Exploited Children had never catalogued. This has been a real positive for the veterans—male and female—as they have helped the government to improve their efforts.

Student Sends Letters of Apology

Lawrence Budd, a staff writer for the *Dayton Daily News*, told the story of how Andrew Stadler, 18, of Springboro sent out 1,000 notes of apology for having posted warnings of bomb threats to his high school. The warning has caused the school to evacuate and be closed while it was searched thoroughly.

His apology was sent to his school mates by the Warren County Prosecutor's Office. "Stadler indicated in the letter that he was despondent at the time and told his classmates not to be afraid to ask for help." Such actions by the Prosecutor (David Fornshell) represent the kind of treatment that is being seen more and more these days. The goal is to turn it into a "learning opportunity" for the entire school and to also provide Andrew with the help he so badly needs.

In addition to the letters, Fornshell also met with class meetings for 9, 10, 11, and 12th graders as he explained the seriousness of the charges, but also the importance of trying to reach out to those with mental problems. Mr. Sadler had at one time been giving serious thought to taking his own life. Each of us is needed to be of help to one another.

77 Named by Seattle Archdiocese as Child Abusers

The Seattle Archdiocese has cited 'Transparency and Accountability" as it has for the first time provided the actual names of 77 persons who were known to be child abusers. An

AP notice printed in the January 17, 2016 issue of the *New York Times* had Archbishop J. Peter Sartain apologizing for this list of names of men who had served or lived in western Washington state over the past several decades.

"Our work in this area will not be complete until all those who have been harmed have received assistance in healing, and until the evil of child sexual abuse has been eradicated from society," the church leader said. Such openness is to be highly valued as it makes the efforts at reform and justice much easier to have.

ACLU Seeks Changes to Ohio's Criminal Laws

In Laura A. Bischoff's March 23, 2016 article published in the *Dayton Daily News* she outlines the sweeping changes in how Ohio approaches crime and punishment. These changes, part of a 17-page report by the ACLU would be a major change in Ohio's system of justice if even half were enacted by the legislature. Among the many suggestions are the following:

- Limit harsh, automatic punishments that take away judicial discretion.
- Make rehabilitation a priority and increase mental health spending.
- Use tickets instead of arresting people accused of non-violent misdemeanor charges.
- Eliminate pay-to-stay jail fees and reduce fines and fees imposed on low-income persons.

- Reduce post prison release punishments that hurt an ex-con's ability to get a job and improve the community control system.

Ohio last re-wrote its entire criminal code in 1971. The Ohio 24-member Criminal Justice Recodification Committee includes prosecutors, defense attorneys, judges, prison officials and others. This is the organization to whom the ACLU report was sent.

Colorado Female Prisoners Training Dogs

Anna Mulrine, a staff writer for the *Christian Science Monitor,* entitled her May 30, 2016 article as follows: "The amazing grace of Unit 1—In one unit of a Colorado prison, female convicts are saving dogs, veterans—and themselves." The Denver Women's Correctional Facility has become a major source of 'trained dogs' because although they have proved their worth to veterans, the costs of training were not covered by insurance or the VA.

Why does it matter? The mental wounds of war can run deep for the vets, mostly male but with a few female as well. But for the female prisoners who train the dogs, the gift brings its own blessings—a sense of unconditional love restored. The program clearly is a vital help to the vets and their families but it also provides the inmates with a reduction in recidivism, a focus on service to others and societal positives.

Paul Sasse, who served in Iraq and Afghanistan and has struggled with post-traumatic stress said, "Sapphire helped our whole family. What the women prisoners do makes a huge, huge difference." He flew to Colorado to pick up his dog, Sapphire, who was in the program because of a woman who lost her husband and wanted to pay the costs to honor him. Sapphire now has her main job, "blocking people for me. I get really uncomfortable when people get too close to me."

"The inmates work with their trainees day and night for six to eight weeks, sleeping with them in their cells and taking them to chow hall to make sure they do not beg for food or dive for dropped scraps." One prisoner observed that people say that we are saving the dogs, but in reality "they are saving us."

U.S. Attorney General Seeks to Ease Re-entry

Eric Tucker of the Associated Press wrote his article about the need for all local, state and federal units to ease re-entry to society after release. Published by the *Dayton Daily News* on April 26, 2016 his work provided many examples of what would help this process. For example, as more and more states now require an ID card for voting and other purposes, Loretta Lynch urged states to make obtaining such a card much easier for the thousands of former inmates who are returning to everyday life each year.

"The long-term impact of a criminal record prevents many people obtaining employment, housing, higher education, and credit…and these barriers affect returning individuals even if they have turned their lives around and are very unlikely to reoffend." She stressed that making these types of changes would provide many with positive assistance.

Harvard Law School's 'Fair Punishment Project'

This new effort was announced on March 30, 2016 in an email to me. It stated, "The Project will use legal research and educational initiatives to ensure that the U.S. justice system is fair and accountable. The Project will work to highlight the gross injustices resulting from prosecutorial misconduct, ineffective defense lawyers, and racial bias and exclusion. We are dedicated to illuminating the laws that result in excessive punishment, especially the death penalty and juvenile life without parole."

The leaders of this new organization see it as a valuable resource for anyone and everyone who seeks to bring about a fair and equitable justice system. They invite such folks to visit their website at www.fairpunishment.org to learn more about their work.

Such a new organization and the work that it is most likely to produce is certain to bring about changes in our justice system. I am certain that the reputation of Harvard and the diligence of the students involved will do much to promote needed changes in this system.

Rewarding Police Officers for Showing Restraint

Erwin Haines Whack, Associate Press, published an article in the *Dayton Daily News* on June 5, 2016 under the lead of Public Safety with the headline: "Police officers rewarded for displaying restraint." Whack addressed the change in Philadelphia, PA when he wrote, "A few police agencies in the U.S. have begun rewarding officers for showing restraint in the line of duty, putting the tactic on par with bravery."

"More than 40 Philadelphia officers have received awards since December for defusing conflicts without shooting, clubbing or otherwise using maximum force against anyone." Following suit for example the Los Angeles Police Department recently created a Preservation of Life Award. "Such awards are key to changing the mentality inside law enforcement," said Phillip Goff, director of the Center for Policing Equity, a think tank.

Rebuilding Lives In Omaha, NE

"A proponent for rebuilding lives in the Douglas County Correctional Center's housing unit for veterans" said Mike Watkins in his story in the October 6, 2016 issue of the *Omaha World Herald.* He continued with identifying Mary Ann Borgeson as that leading proponent. The program (It's) "the first rehabilitation program of its kind for inmates in Nebraska and one of about a dozen in county jails nationwide."

"Open to all incarcerated male veterans who meet intake criteria, the military-structured unit is…laser-focused on helping those with post-traumatic stress disorder (PTSO), mental health issues, and other life challenges. Borgeson is a member of the County Commission who has championed the program. She "salutes a select group of inmates for contributing to the final unit layout and day's structure…We wanted to this to be by them as well as for them."

The Prison Coders

Ann Scott Tyson's cover story for the *Christian Science Monitor*'s November 28, 2016 issue is headlined, "San Quentin inmates train as software engineers, part of a push in the U.S. to prepare prisoners for life on the 'outside.'" Schuhmacher, a prisoner for the last 16 years, is paid $16.77 per hour compared to the usual prison wages of less that $1.00 per hour. "And he likes it---back in his cell at night he roughs out answers to coding problems with pen and paper. But most important is what the work will offer Schumacher once he gets out: a sense of purpose and the possibility of starting a new life."

Schuhmacher says, "I know my crime was super violent, but I've used my time in prison to my advantage." Others have earned college degrees and one is now a certified sheet metal worker who may be released quite soon. "He will go on parole and live in transitional housing that provides meals and health care. He also has a job waiting at the San Francisco firm Rocket Space, which runs a technology campus for start ups. After 19 years of prison, I'm prepared for anything."

"Ban the Box" = Second Chance

The General Counsel and Senior Vice President of Koch Industries, Mark Holden wrote an opinion piece for the *Omaha World-Herald* on November 20, 2016 in which he outlined the need for banning the box on employment application forms. The "BOX" has been the one to be checked for all potential employees to indicate whether or not they had ever been incarcerated for a felony.

It seems that Congress may not pass this action, but clearly states to his Husker readers, that "the roughly 39,000 employers that call Nebraska home can consider voluntarily taking action themselves." This would give all prisoners the chance to make their own case before an employer as to his (or her) skills, experience, work habits, etc. It would allow them to make their own case and to have their employment decision be made on who they now are, not on what they once were!

This is a major move for Koch Industries to make in that they have the reputation for being very conservative and yet here is their General Counsel making this very safe and business-like proposal. Thousands of current and former felons will deeply appreciate such a chance!

This move to Ban the Box is a very significant one for businesses and colleges in order to give ex-cons more of a chance to make their case and to be hired. It is such a simple action to take, yet it has much potential.

$2 Lab Kit Unreliable—Cases Dismissed Later

The cover story of the *New York Times Magazine* of 7-10-2016 featured a full page letter from Marie Munier, Assistant District Attorney in Harris (Houston) County, Texas with Devon Anderson as the District Attorney. Ryan Gabrielson and Topher Sanders were the co-authors of this major story which included this comment on the front cover; "A flawed drug test could be sending thousands of innocent people to jail each year. Why are police departments and prosecutors still using it?"

The actual letter's first paragraph said that, "the Laboratory Report in your case shows that the evidence tested negative for a controlled substance. A copy of your lab report is attached to this letter." The next paragraph was even more telling: **"Accordingly, you were prosecuted for a criminal drug offense and convicted in error."** It then went on to inform the men and women receiving this letter that they could take action to have this criminal conviction removed and then how to go about doing this.

The problem was that this $2.00 testing packet was being given by untrained police and rarely, if ever, actually having a Laboratory Test done on the results. People caught in this trap were told they could spend a few weeks in jail or two years in prison. Most opted for the short jail time believing that the test was valid even though they had not had any of the controlled substances.

Now with the real testing having been completed after much pushing by the prosecutors, they were being informed of this wonderful news. This prosecutorial action represents the good news and the solid evidence of what a small change within the justice system can do!

Fair Punishment Project: 2 Suggestions

Two specific suggestions have been developed by this Harvard Law School project to make quick and needed changes in our U.S. Justice System for youth offenders. Both were published on March 24, 2016. **Life With Out**

Parole (LWOP) is still practiced in some places with just five counties accounting for more that 20% of all juvenile LWOP sentences. Philadelphia alone accounts for 9% of all such sentences.

The studies of this form of solitary confinement with no hope of ever being released from it resulted in two key findings: "1. JLWOP sentences are largely imposed by a handful of outlier counties and states, and 2. JLWOP is disproportionately imposed on persons of color."

The second set of findings regarding juvenile justice focused on **From Bad Lawyers to No Lawyer at All.** "The quality of attorneys providing a defense to individuals charged with crimes that expose them to possible life without parole sentences varies tremendously. Some are not up to the extremely important task of providing a vigorous defense after conducting a thorough investigation."

Whether these lawyers were unqualified, under-resourced, or just plain uninterested, those that fit into any or all of these categories fail fundamentally to comprehend and make their clients aware of the seriousness of the charges they face. Our system of justice can be improved dramatically by making sure that neither of these situations can continue to exist in the U.S.

Local Courts' Diversion Program

Mary Beth Lane writing for the *Columbus Dispatch* on June 4, 2016 highlights a very positive way to reduce the population of our jails and prisons while ALSO serving its community and the potential inmates. The Athens County

(OH) Prosecutor Keller Blackburn has a diversion program and four women before the court had been convicted and sentenced but none will have to face 'time' if they follow the diversion plan.

"If we can treat the addiction while making victims whole and rehabilitating the offender, and the offender can have no criminal record at the end of it, the societal benefits are great," said Blackburn. The four women are among nearly 200+ which requires such participation as an alternative to being locked up.

The Ohio Prosecuting Attorneys Association doesn't track how many of its members have diversion programs but those that do seem to be working very well. When incarceration costs are saved, addictions and related problems are addressed, then we are much more likely to have a person ready for full release back into society. And we have saved the taxpayers a lot of their precious dollars as a result. "These programs seem to work well," said OPAA Executive Director John Murphy.

Sex Offender Laws Being Changed

The editorial on September 8, 2015 in the *New York Times* led with the headline, "Banishing Sex Offenders Doesn't Help," and then proceeded to support that with many facts. The distorted versions of this offence have led to paranoia that has led the federal government and local governments to create a mass of laws and restrictions that violate the Constitution and make punishment continue for years—even for life in some cases.

Lately the courts have begun to attack some of these situations. "The California Supreme Court…holding that a San Diego residency restriction which effectively barred paroled sex offenders from 97 percent of available housing, violated the United States Constitution." The Sixth Circuit Court attacked the Michigan law very directly for its many restrictions of life long after parole was over. The editorial concluded, "It is understandable to want to do everything possible to protect children from being abused. But not all people who have been convicted of sex offenses pose a risk to children, if they pose any risk at all."

While this type of action was dealt with previously, but its vital importance to many ex-inmates is vital and it deserves a reminder in this chapter.

Keeping Kids From Crime

Stacy Teicher Khadaroo wrote this cover story for the February 16, 2015 issue of the *Christian Science Monitor* (CSM) with the above title and this following cover Headline. "How an alternative to lockups—a 'continuum of care'—is changing juvenile justice." Her article focuses upon Toledo (Lucas County), OH in great detail but similar programs do exist elsewhere in Ohio and beyond for sure.

When a youth is first arrested in Lucas County (and in Montgomery County: Dayton) he or she is taken first to the local juvenile facility for a thorough assessment. That process includes school work, activities, health (both mental and physical), etc. When all those essential pieces of information are known, then the decisions about possible incarceration are made. "You can send a kid away to juvenile prison for six months or a year, but guess what, he's coming back. And if you've increased his criminality…then you've increased the risk to the community;" said Deborah Hodges, a Lucas County Juvenile Court Administrator.

"Still for many of the kids who are locked up, the experience poses more risk to them than the risk they pose to the community, advocates for de-incarceration say. One in 10 confined youths surveyed said he or she had been sexually abused by staff or other youth and 42 percent feared physical attack" according to a 2011 report by the Annie E. Casey Foundation.

In Montgomery County (Dayton) Ohio the same kind of results have also reduced the crime rate, the number of kids who have successfully finished school with a regular or a GED diploma have increased. The Youth Drug Court there has also been very successful and returned many adolescents back to their homes with much stronger skills and work habits—truly prepared for life.

Tara Hobbs, administrator of the Lucas County (Ohio) Youth Treatment Center summed up the program this way: "They've unfortunately made choices that harmed others, but that doesn't take away that they deserve to be helped, too, AND healed." In this kind of a plan for youth a major step has been taken to remove a major step in the school-to-prison pipeline!

Conclusion

There are many reasons for this chapter to be placed here near the end of this book. The most important is to provide the reader with dozens of ways in which people, groups, citizens, leaders, officers, media, and others are already making changes in our judicial system.

I want to encourage all of you to do your part in supporting them and making our system one which truly serves ALL people. The next and final chapter is post-election of 2016 and it is not as hopeful.

CHAPTER 16

2017 The Future?

This nation is now well into many months of a new administration with President Trump already into major problems and storm clouds arising rapidly. He is unable to recruit hundreds of staff to fill the open vacancies throughout his administration. He has had a number of potential appointments withdraw before even standing for a confirmation vote.

Much alarm has been raised about President Trump's appointments, budgets, tax reforms, and other statements and actions that the badly needed reform of our judicial system will be able to continue to move ahead. This chapter is an attempt to look at some elements of the current landscape in our society to see how our justice system is able to adjust to the new reality.

(Sunday Review The New York Times, 3-26-2017, p. 1+.) Headline: "Justice Springs Eternal: Donald Trump's presidency doesn't spell the end of criminal justice reform. It may just be getting started."

The world seems to be having many problems with trying to determine just what, if any, real United States policy or position may be for dealing with world issues such as ISIS, climate, and international problems. Confusing tweets further confuse almost every issue from minor ones such as attendance at the inauguration to such major ones as the immigration bans on Muslims coming to this country add to the standstill congress.

(TIME, 6-19-17, p., 15) "CLAIM After the London attacks, Trump called Senate Democrats 'obstructionists' for holding up his political nominees, 'including ambassadors.' REALITY Trump hasn't nominated an ambassador to the U.K. or anyone to fill 426 other federal jobs requiring Senate sign-off. There are 112 open political slots at the State Department." With Education and Justice among those departments not filling job positions, actions are being delayed.

(The Nation, 6-30-17) Headline: "The Trump Administration's Voter-Suppression Plans Are Backfiring Badly" In an unprecedented show of bipartisan resistance, 45 states are refusing to hand over private voter data.." Most notable has been some strong opposition from Republicans who have refused to send such data as requested. Such is the effort to preserve our right to vote as an essential human right.

Not long after the Attorney General position was taken by Jeff Sessions, he sent an order for all federal prosecutors to now follow the exact mandates of the law for all charges and sentencing they would seek in the future. He also filed appeals to the several cases where Trumps' Immigration Ban had been banned. He has challenged court rulings with a number of cities and their police departments. He also has challenged several court cases regarding voting rights in such states as Texas and North Carolina.

The overall picture has been very much in contrast to the major movement in judicial reform over the past years. However, the situation has been less of a problem than it seemed at first. The decisions between cities and the Justice Department are being monitored by the Courts involved and the cities have welcomed the guidance involved. The election laws have been upheld very specifically by the U.S. Supreme Court and orders to make revisions in districts are still in effect.

(Baltimore Sun, 4-4-17, by Kevin Rector and Luke Broadwater) The headline read was, "Baltimore leaders pledge police reform will occur with or without consent decree."

(USA Today, 4-10-17, by Kevin Johnson) The headline: "Courts must clear attempts to roll back police pacts." Called for actions are not being enforced and thus attempts to roll back justice reforms are being delayed as well."

(The Nation, 4-11-17, by Eri Berman) Headlines: "A Big Win for Voting Rights in Texas and a Big Loss for Trump; *Rebuking Jeff Sessions, a federal court rules that Texas's voter-10 law intentionally discriminated against minority voters."*

MSNBC-TV broadcast announcer reports: The Court confirmed its approval of the North Carolina Appeal Court's decision by a 5-3 vote which included quietly conservative Justice Thomas siding with the majority! This decision outlawed the "strategically surgical actions" which allowed the discrimination.

(USA Today, 6-20-17, by Richard Wolf, p 8) "Justices will weigh in on politics, partisan gerrymandering" This case is similar to the situation in Ohio, Florida, Michigan, North Carolina, Pennsylvania, and Virginia.

While there have been more calls from local prosecutors around the nation recently for treating juveniles accused of murder or attempted murder to be moved to adult court for trials, there have also been many cautions against such practice becoming 'ordinary'. Even with the Trump emphasis of 'law and order' being given much coverage by the media, congress has not jumped on his band-wagon for this negative movement downward.

(The Hill, 4-4-17, by Owen Eagan) Headline: "House panel approves bills on juvenile justice, missing children." "A House panel on Tuesday advanced two bills with bi-partisan support aimed at improving the welfare of missing and exploited children and reforming the juvenile justice system... that includes education and rehabilitation efforts."

Major attention on the overcrowded and poorly-managed prison systems in our nation have been receiving much public notice via the press this past year. Because such needed reforms are, themselves, costly and difficult to obtain, progress has been slow given the current new federal administration. But there does remain hope at least in some cases nationwide.

(Omaha World-Herald, 3-26-17 Editorial) Headline+ "Nebraksa Prisons: Don't derail progress. "...The numbers are starting to turn around because all three branches of state government are engaged on prison reforms." The rehabilitative approach promises to benefit both public safety and the public purse by giving inmates the tools to succeed in the community, reducing recidivism." local voters are informing crucial decisions.

(KIFY 10 News, 3-23-17) Headline: "Louisiana eyes overhaul of its criminal justice system."

A clear focus of needed justice system reform has been on changes in the "bail system" which in too many locations (Louisiana for example) has become a "debtor prison" system of raising local cash for the local budgets and a way of increasing incarceration. Numerous stories have been reported of people pleading guilty to a minor crime because they could get reduced jail time in exchange for not having to pay their bail bond fees.

(Christian Science Monitor Weekly, 4-10-17, by Nissa Rhee) Headlines: "Has US bail reform hit a tipping point? Facing lawsuits and tight budgets, states are rethinking the concept of money bonds." "WHY IT MATTERS The US Justice Department estimates that 450,000 Americans are stuck in limbo every day, imprisoned before their day in court..." Debtor prisons are now being challenged.

(The New York Times, 4-30-17, by Eli Rosenberg) Headline: "Judge in Houston Strikes Down County's Bail System, Saying It's Unfair to the Poor." "The ruling, part of a civil rights lawsuit against the county...a woman was arrested on a charge of driving without a license...could not post $2,500 in bail. local voters are being made aware of existing problems."

Our nation has been slowly trying to reduce its world-leading role as a nation of peoples who have been incarcerated. Closing private prisons has been an action being taken recently as both states and federal governments have seen the costs involved and the poor results of such massive 'non-state control' of prisons. This is an area where continued reductions are much in question.

(The Washington Post, 3-24-17, by David Makamura) Headline: "Blame game: Trump casts immigrants as dangerous criminals, but the evidence shows otherwise" While the Courts have slowed down the 'ban process', the arrest and deportation of others already here in the US including the "dreamers" has been moving along swiftly. The article closes with a quote, "I see it as a political tactic to support a policy agenda. It's policymaking by fear, not fact."

(The New York Times, 3-5-17, Sunday Editorial) "Statehouse Politics Embarrass the Nation" Wisconsin has just cut its parole agency staff from eight employees to just one. This was designed to make sure that some 2000 inmates now eligible for a release, instead must continue to serve out their full term. "Some Republican ideas: make jail more likely for protestors and parole harder to attain."

(Dayton Daily News, 3-26-17, by Matt Zapotosky p. A21} Headlines: Justice Department says it still needs private prisons. Federal inmate population down 14% since 2013. AG Sessions has his own 'plan' in disregard of such 'fake news.'

(USA TODAY, 3-22-2017, by Ryan Martin, p. SB) "Every Indiana inmate soon could have own tablet...They can be used for learning and help families stay connected, but there is potential for abuse."

Among the most important aspects of the reform of our judicial system has been finding ways to improve an inmates return to a quality life among society. One way to help this job seeking process was to "ban the box" which too often was a part of the ex-inmates' application forms for a job, college entrance, etc. With box gone, acknowledging ones past offense and punishment was delayed until the person had a chance to be interviewed first. Often this was found to improve the opportunity for a job, college attendance, etc.

But with the results of the election, such efforts were among the first to be discarded by some employers and even by some colleges. Given this discouraging downturn, this short story is seen as a very positive signal that 'ban the box' may still be active.

(The Christian Science Monitor, 4-24\5-1, p. 33} Headline: "Redemption for ex offenders who stay clean." The article goes on to state that "More than 30 percent of the American adult population has a criminal record, making it difficult for them to work, go to school, or receive government benefits...People need not be defined by past mistakes if amends are made-and then forgiveness is forthcoming in the form of a second chance...and their recidivism goes down."

(USA Today, 4-20-17, p. SA, by Fatima Hussain) Headline: "Rights groups urge veto of Ind. bill on criminal pasts." Twelve civic organizations want to stop Indiana's governor from signing a bill...20 states now limit such boxes."

A major problem within our justice system has been the frequent lack of openness and transparency by local public law officials and their communities following police-citizen killings. Progress was being made and more cameras are now worn by local officers but recent court decisions of "not guilty" (Officer Jeronimo Yanez was exonerated by the Minnesota court but fired by his local police department) provoked more protests. In Cincinnati, where the courts are retrying the ex-University of Cincinnati officer for the killing of Samuel DuBose, there is much attention being given.

The New York Times, 6-18-17, p. 13 by Mitch Smith, Vamicher Alcindo and Jack Bailey.) Headlines: "Grim Echoes for Families: Officer Shoots and Jury Acquits. A pattern in which few officers are charged and fewer still convicted." Given the impact of such actions/events, it is clear that the need for much more work of genuine law enforcement openness remains a prime goal for justice reform.

Among the many suggestions for reform has been the major need for much retraining for our nation's local and state law enforcement personnel. They are now the 'first-responders' to encounter both adults and children with significant mental health problems. But they are also without any serious preparation as to just how best to deal with persons with such mental health problems. This is a major need of the past but is only recognized by the current press.

(Omaha World-Herald, 6-11-17, p. 1+, by Andrew Nelson and Mark Klecker) Headlines: "Police as 'front-line responders' to mentally ill in crisis. Experts weigh in on training, use of Tasers during encounters that are becoming a daily occurrence for many officers." "The primary goal: De-escalate the situation."

(SPLC Report, Spring 2017, p.4) Headline: SPLC trial over lack of mental health treatment in Alabama prisons concludes." The Southern Poverty Law Center has continued its work on bringing justice to the medical treatment of prisoners in this case in Alabama. Rulings on the several cases brought by SPLC are expected later this year.

Both local police and prison personnel need training to help them deal with events where an individual with mental health problems is involved with them. This need grows as our population ages and mental health problem become even more dominant.

Education has been a major focus of the reform of our judicial system with particular emphasis on the opportunities or lack thereof within the penal system. This has not seemed to be a major emphasis of the new administration except as budget issues may yet call for even less attention. But the quality of our nations pK-12 public schools has taken a dramatic hit with the '50-50 VP Pence vote' putting into the cabinet as Education Secretary, Betsy DeVoss.

Her total personal experience was within only the private, charter schools and their problems with admitting/serving pupils with special needs or problems. Thus this aspect of education remains a significant element of judicial reform.

(The Christian Science Monitor, 4-10-17, by Stacy Teicher Khadaroo, p. 17) Headlines: "Four ways to improve US schools: Public-school-champions and school-choice advocates tend to agree on these steps." "1. Prepare students for college and careers. 2. Start learning early. 3.Don't measure schools (or kids or teachers) only by test scores. 4. Focus on the neediest schools."

(Americans United, 3-16-17, by Maggie Garrett) Headlines: "Wall of Separation: Here's The Skinny: Trump's Trying To Push A Voucher Plan On Us." The Trump plan would cut the Department of Education's budget by 13.5 percent...At the same time the budget would funnel $250 million of taxpayer dollars into a private school voucher program.." Areas for worry are still in the works!

{SPLC Report, Spring 2017, p.4} Headline: "Teaching Tolerance responds to election's negative impact." The SPLC education publication has shifted its coverage to include very explicit helps for teachers to use in countering the huge misgivings by students who must deal with the hate and misinformation being directed at them.

These problems of helping reduce the many problems facing children in our schools to avoid the 'school to prison' pipeline still exist. One solution has been to provide quality preschool experiences for many more children especially those from poor families in the urban area. In Dayton,OH this has been done by City government and was reported in the Nov. 6, 2017 edition of the Dayton Dailey News with the full page headline, "Preschool Promise program *grows.*"

Sex offenders have often been denied their constitutional rights while they have been incarcerated and then even after they have served their sentences. Being denied full access to social sites has been tested in courts and they have begun to rule against this basic right of these prisoners and former prisoners.

(USA TODAY, 6-20-17, p SA by Richard Wolf) Headline: "Ruling: Sex offenders can access social sites. Justices: North Carolina law violates First Amendment."

(The Atlantic, 3-23-17, by Garrett Epps) Headlines: "The Supreme Court Confronts Racism in the Jury Room... Is racism in deliberations any less toxic than racism in open Court?" At least there is this hope for the future of less racism in our judicial system. Conservative Chief Justice Roberts in his opinion in *Buck v. Davis* wrote, "Some toxins can be deadly in small *doses.*"

The topic of juvenile justice has received much attention and some excellent actions over the past several years. Much more data on the adolescent brain and its ability to understand the complexity of so many of the situations in which juveniles find themselves has recently been shared. Two recent citations from 2017 explore significant elements of this section of our justice system.

(The New York Times,3-12-17, Sunday Editorial,p.8) Headlines: "Crime and the Adolescent Brain...New York and North Carolina still try 16-year olds as adults, an inhumane practice that undermines public safety."

(Louisiana Politics and Government,4-18-17, by Julia O'Donoghue,NOLA.com) Headline: "Louisiana takes another look at sentencing juveniles to life without parole." A common practice in many locations to avoid a death sentence but ensure a life behind bars for youthful offenders.

Education issues continue to draw attention. The Nov. *3,* 2017 issue of the Dayton Daily News had a major story on Caring for foster children where court appointed advocates help kids. Written by Beth Anspach, it makes the key point that such care for foster children helps many avoid the prison path totally and leads to youth who are ready for a positive adulthood.

Conclusion

Our nation's effort to make significant revisions to our Judicial System so that it is truly "FOR ALL" as our Pledge of

Allegiance concludes is a vital goal for which I am working. The objective is most worthy of our past efforts and is also in need of our continued work on its many fronts. From voting fairness and equal juries to improved law enforcement training and practices including improved treatment of mental health issues-- the road is not without challenge.

Improving our PK-12 Education system so as to eliminate the "school to prison" element must be included along with better education opportunities for inmates. Such attention to learning at ALL levels is vital. "Ban the box" will improve the chances for good work for released inmates and help them become taxpaying employees in a contributing manner which saves our tax dollars.

To bring this about calls for much work and attention to details throughout our system. It means we must be alert to the current efforts to restrict justice, inhibit public schools, punish rather that help those with mental health problems, and restrict the right to be an active voter in our society. I have tried to show all of these problems throughout this book and now it is up to the readers to become watch dogs for our justice system.

There is much to do and it will need the concerted effort of all parts of our society working together in order to make this happen. My goal is so see all schools having their students being able to recite the Pledge and to be very proud when they bring it to its conclusion because it will mean that all of their peers do have access to a genuine system which is a Justice for All in our own nation!

Printed in the United States
By Bookmasters